Cooking the Once a Month Way

A complete guide and 6 month menu

Volume 1

Written and Published By:

Jamiee Wade

Cooking the Once a Month Way
A complete guide and 6 month menu
Volume 1

FIRST EDITION – November 2013

Includes Index

ISBN: 978-0615915630

Printed and Produced by:

CreateSpace, an Amazon company.

Thank you for picking up this book. You may be overworked, over scheduled or simply not a good cook. This book will help you simplify your daily, weekly and monthly meal planning. It aims to help you save money and time in the kitchen. If you don't approach cooking with the once a month method in mind, you will hopefully gain some new knowledge about how to streamline kitchen time. More importantly for most of us, you will gain new, delicious recipes to try with your family!

Use my knowledge and experience to bring your family back to the table and make your life easier and more delicious!

Dedication

I want to dedicate this book to my family and friends who, through their work and support, made this book possible.

Table of Contents

Who we are and why we started doing <u>Once a Month cooking</u>

Each family that uses a method such as once a month cooking has their own story as to why they started cooking this way. Let me tell you my story and the story of 2 of my dear friends.

In 2002 I was pregnant with my 2nd child and knew that I needed to make a change in how our family handled dinner. Many times, because of my pregnancy and my 3 year old, I would not prepare for dinner early enough in the day – including not defrosting meat or even thinking of what to fix. Often times because of this lack of preplanning we would either eat out, eat late or eat non-dinner things for dinner, like cold sandwiches or cereal.

My dear friend, Cindy Schouten, introduced me to a book *Once a Month Cooking* by Mimi Wilson and MaryBeth Lageborg. I read this book, showed to another friend who had just had her second baby and was returning to work. We both decided we should try this book and see if it truly would simplify our lives and help our families eat better plus save us money and time.

The first time we did once a month cooking was January 1, 2003. I did the grocery shopping a couple of days previously and had everything laid out when Jennifer arrived. Amazingly, it took us over 10 hours to do our first round of cooking, which included 15 recipes. After that day, we weren't sure we really wanted to do this again, but we wanted to discuss it again after we ate some meals and saw how the month went.

The first month went fabulously! I could defrost a dinner the night before and pop it in the oven, set a timer and go out to play with my daughter. The meals were large enough that we had leftovers later that week – this meant even less time in the kitchen for me and our dollars were stretched even farther, we often had 2 meals (or more) out of one entree.

Jennifer's family had the same experience, but better. Jennifer worked full time and arrived home later than her husband, so in the morning she would set the food out to defrost and her husband could come home and easily prepare dinner without any work or fuss. Instead of eating frozen prepared meals, they were eating frozen meals that she had prepared for them! So she was saving calories, salt and most importantly MONEY!

At the end of January we talked and evaluated the preparation method, choice of recipes and other things. The most important topic we discussed was if this type of cooking simplified our lives, both families wholeheartedly agreed that it did. Even though it took a long time, once a month, it saved time and money over the entire month. In addition, our husbands were thrilled with a hot, unique dinner each night. We all appreciated that dinner was on the table sooner and clean up after dinner was super-fast and easy – only a couple of plates, forks, cups, knives and 1 or 2 pans, depending on the meal! Clean up took less than 10 minutes, which means more family time (and less clean up time)!

We had successfully brought our families back to the dinner table. We had saved ourselves time and most importantly we fed them healthy, tasty dishes. Most importantly we saved our families a lot of money!

After using the book by Mimi Wilson and MaryBeth Legaborg for a few months, we both understood the types of recipes that could be chosen and used. Plus we knew how to alter recipes so that they could be semi-prepared and frozen, then defrosted and heated. So we broke out and started picking out recipes from our own cookbooks and doing them each month. We also learned a lot of short cuts, so that the preparation and assembly time took less and less time each month. After about six round of once a month cooking, we had the preparation and assembly time down to about three hours for 15 meals.

Each month our preparation time got shorter and shorter as we learned tricks and shortcuts, which we will teach you in this book. Also, our menu varieties got broader and broader. We didn't love every recipe that we chose, but we consistently chose different ones so that we could offer different meals to our families. The recipes in this book have been tried many times by many families, so you don't have to go through the same growth we did!

Jennifer and I kept up our once a month cooking, actually more like every 6 weeks cooking, for over 2 years. Then I met another friend, Vicki and she decided to join us.

Cooking for 3 families is actually easier and cheaper than just 1 or 2 families - also it is more fun. More hands make the work lighter. By having 3 people doing the recipes, we could each take 5 recipes and prepare them and we were done with assembly in about 3 hours, then we would spend an hour cleaning up.

Vicki joined us because she was so busy with her kids. She is also a stay at home mom, but is always running with her kids to activities and church and school stuff. Beyond that, Vicki does not like to cook; in fact, she avoids it at all costs. Her family was eating out many times a week and when they weren't eating out, they were doing simple barbecuing or having a pre-prepared meal from the freezer. This simply was not healthy for their bodies or their pocket book. The first month took a little bit of getting use to the different recipes for her family, but now, 3 years later they love it and the kids even help out!

Our story continues by association. 2 friends heard what we did and they asked to join – so we are up to 5 families. We did this for a month and decided that 5 isn't the perfect number, let's try 10. So we moved up to 10 families and that was the perfect number! We could set up 5 workstations with 2 people at each place. Each station would then assemble 3 recipes each for each team member. For example team 1 would prepare Chicken a la Sheila 10 times and then they would prepare their next two meals. This was while the other 4 teams were each preparing their 3 meals. By the end of the cooking session, each person had 15 delicious meals to take home, but only worked on 3. You didn't feel overwhelmed and you had a fun afternoon with friends.

The cost with 10 families went down incredibly! Originally 15 meals for 2 families would cost each family approximately $175. When we increased to 3 families, the cost went down, but not by much. Increasing to 10 families, the cost for the same 15 meals decreased to around $100. The reason the cost went down was because we could buy in bigger bulk and receive a better discount from a large warehouse store. Plus we could buy canned items in the huge restaurant style cans, versus the small ones you buy at the grocery store. By streamlining the process and having different stations, the assembly time was reduced to about two hours and about thirty to forty-five minutes of clean up.

We were able to ease our preparation too by contacting a food service supply company. I realize this type of company is not available in all areas, but if you are in a major metropolitan area, you can often take advantage of their products and services. The prices hardly ever vary, the quality is extremely consistent. More importantly to me, we could buy chicken breasts that were a consistent size – 4 or 6 ounce, instead of having a variety of size chicken breasts in the frozen bag from the large warehouse store. Furthermore, I could buy precooked, cut up chicken breasts for casseroles. This cut our preparation time down tremendously! I could even buy meat already cut up for stir-fry and save us preparation time.

We could almost always buy our canned goods from our food service representative. They sell industrial size food products that are used in restaurants and other food locations. The cans are called #10 cans and they contain between six and seven pounds of food, such as stewed tomatoes, beans or corn. We also purchase most seasonings and liquid sauces, such as soy sauce and Worcestershire sauce, in 1 gallon containers. This may seem like a lot, but if you are making 10 sets of a recipe, you will often go through 1 gallon or more of a sauce. Not only does buying from a food service company save money, but it also can save the environment – you have less packaging and waste than buying conventional cans of food.

Now, a few years later, I am able to share my wealth of knowledge with you. I truly hope that you and your family can benefit from my experience and knowledge so you don't have to go through the same learning curve we did. I pray that you too can bring your family back to the table and enjoy more time with you family and less time in the kitchen!

Benefits of Once a Month cooking

There are so many benefits to this type of cooking. Because each family receives different benefits I will list the most popular benefits, as I have experienced them and heard from friends.

Saves Money

Before I started once a month cooking, we would eat out two or three times a week. Each dinner out cost us between twenty and forty dollars. Even going to fast food, was over ten dollars a trip. Add this up and multiply by four weeks in a month and my food budget increased by over $300 and that wasn't for every day groceries! That's an extra vacation a year or a small car payment or even paying off an extra bill!

In addition, if I forgot to create a weekly menu, I would often run to the grocery store two or three times a week. Again, this was increasing my monthly grocery bill. You know when you go to the store hungry and with a small child you never get out with just what you came for. You nearly always spend twice the amount you think. So there I was, running up another bill, instead of being a good steward with our money. By having the meals in the freezer, we were able to decrease eating out to once a week or even once every other week. We could now choose when we went out to eat, instead of being forced in to eating out because I had nothing prepared.

By doing once a month cooking and doing it with my friends, I was able to spend about $100 a month for 15 entrees. Each entrée in this book feeds 6-8 adults. With only 2 adults and 2 children at home, each entrée stretched to more than one meal, so we saved even more money and time.

Helping Others

One of the best benefits of this type of cooking is being able to help your friends. Many times I have friends call me and tell me that someone in their home is sick or they are having a horrid day. Because I have a meal in the freezer, I can pull it out and either take it over frozen, or cook it and take it over and help that family or friend out. People love your hospitality, graciousness and you get a wonderful feeling from helping out others.

Saves Time

Before approaching once a month cooking, I would spend about an hour or two a week at the grocery store. Each afternoon I would spend anywhere from 30 minutes to an hour preparing dinner; then add the cook time. After eating, we would have to clean up, which would take about 30 minutes. So daily, I would spend about 1 to 2 hours making dinner and cleaning up. This was time that I couldn't spend with my small children or my husband.

Once a month cooking changed my shopping, prep and clean up time. Shopping would take about 2-3 hours for the entire month's meals. Creating the meals would take 3-5 hours, plus an hour for clean-up. So I would spend about 10 hours, one day a month, making a month's worth of meals. That alone is a huge time savings.

The next savings was my daily time. Every other day, I set out a meal and let it defrost all day and then pop it on the stove or in the oven. No time at all out of my day. Clean-up is a breeze! We have our plates, silverware and possibly 3 pans – one for the entrée, a side and one for vegetables and that is ALL! Clean up takes about 10 minutes. This leaves more time for family or whatever I prefer to do.

Weight Control or Weight Loss

I find when I am cooking from scratch that I snack a lot and then notice the extra pounds when I am getting dressed. When I started this cooking method, I found that I couldn't snack while cooking – the meal was prepared and ready for the oven (as in a casserole) or it was raw and in a bag and I wouldn't touch it until it was done.

In addition, because we were using consistent size chicken breasts from the food supplier, I knew that I would eat the right size portion of meat. This helped me lose weight as I was no longer eating just what I served myself, which could be a 10 ounce chicken breast, but was a consistent 4 ounce chicken breast.

Expands your Eating Repertoire

This next benefit is a bit different, but most cooks can relate. Before starting this type of cooking, I owned about 50 cookbooks. However, I had a repertoire of 10 recipes that I would make over and over. Some were delicious, some were seriously boring. Dinner was not a highlight of the day. By doing once a month cooking, I opened myself up to finding new recipes to try each month. Favorites would resurface and non-favorites would go away. Each chapter in this book has fourteen unique recipes; there are no recipe repeats through the book.

Involve family members in dinner preparation

Once you have assembled and frozen the meal, half the meal is done! Many times non-cooking spouses refuse to make dinner because the instructions are confusing to them. The cooking instructions in this book are so simple and straight forward that your husband or teenager can prepare dinner if you are sick, busy, working or are out and about! There is no excuse for someone else not making dinner.

Co-oping – the Whys and Hows

I have talked to many people who have done once a month-style cooking. Many have told me that they quit after the first month or two of doing it alone. They see the money and time savings over all, but the time investment to do the preparation was overwhelming to them.

Truly, I almost quit after the first month – remember the first round of cooking that my friend Jennifer and I did took over 10 hours and this was after about three hours of grocery shopping! I thought – this is ridiculous and painful; however, after enjoying the meals all month, I knew I could do this again and learn from the 1st month's mistakes and make the process go faster.

This book will teach you how to be efficient time and moneywise, so it doesn't take you 10 hours to do your cooking. If you want to save even more time and money, you will want to consider doing a co-op or group session.

Yes, I know the objections – I don't have the space, I don't know how to set it up, how do I get the food and store it before everyone gets here. This section will hopefully allay all those concerns and fears and before long, you and your friends will be eating less expensively and healthier than you ever have before!

I have done the co-op or group cooking for about 3 years. The first few months were rocky, but after working out the kinks, I know I can share my wisdom with you and help you avoid many of the pitfalls I fell in to.

First of all – if you go to a meal assembly store you will independently move around the store and assemble your own meals and go home. The way I suggest doing a co-op or group is not this way. You will have up to 5 stations set up and have 1 or 2 people working at each station to assemble 2 or 3 meals for each family. If you have less than 10 people in your group, or a smaller space, choose how many stations you want to set up. You will want a maximum of 2 people working at each station, otherwise people will run in to each other and people get confused on what ingredients have and have not been added.

When setting up each station, consider what recipes might flow together and make it easier to assemble. For example, I put the hamburger recipes at one station, plus 1 other beef. I will typically put 3 chicken recipes at another station. Because there are 14 recipes per chapter, if you set up five stations, you will have one station with only two recipes. That station usually has the pork and vegetarian recipe, when I set up my stations.

Here's a real example: with 10 families in your group you will want to set up 5 stations, with two people working each station. Station 1 will have 2 workers where they will assemble 10 sets of Chicken a la Sheila, then 10 sets of King Ranch Casserole, then 10 sets of Chicken Chili Verde. Station 2 will have 2 other workers. They will assemble 10 sets of Wild Rice and Chicken Casserole, then 10 sets of Chicken Breasts in Mustard Sauce and finally 10 sets of Sunshine Chicken. The other 3 stations will do the other meals.

Each station will be supplied with the ingredients to make their recipes. However, you will share seasonings – there is no reason to buy 5 bottles of any seasonings, except for chopped garlic, possibly. If possible, buy the largest container of liquid or dry seasoning you can – for example, 1 gallon soy sauce or industrial size container of taco seasoning. If you are co-oping with friends, you will often go through at least a gallon of certain liquid seasonings, such as soy sauce, in a cooking session.

You will need to invest a little in equipment if you are going to co-op. I went to a local large store and purchased 5 plastic, 18 quart, wash tubs, 5 sets of measuring cups, 5 sets of measuring spoons and 5 sets of spoons and 2 or 3 ladles. You don't have to spend a lot of money to get these items; I purchased the least expensive measuring cups and spoons.

You will want 18 quart or slightly larger wash tubs so that you can mix large quantities in them – for example, any of the meatloaf recipes, Taco Twist or any of the mixed casseroles. Regular, home size bowls simply don't work when you are working with 10-15 pounds of hamburger at a time. Many months you will only use the tubs for one recipe, but other months, you will use all 5 of them.

The first concern that I have heard is, "Where do I do this or is my kitchen large enough?" Some people do have large enough kitchens and some don't. Really look at your space and see how many people and "stations" you can set up. A station is where 1 or 2 people work at a time assembling meals. My kitchen has a decent amount of counter space; however, to set up five stations, we use 3 different counter top areas, a kitchen table and a 6' folding table. Each counter top area only needs to be a minimum of three feet long to be a station. The smaller workstations can be cozy with two people working at them, but you learn quickly just to have fun being cozy.

To set up, each station will have spices, some #10 cans (detailed later), a plastic, 18 quart wash tub and measuring equipment. Typically, I set the meat on the floor, in their boxes if there is no room on the counter. If your food is in a box or bag that is unopened, there is no problem with contamination by sitting on the floor. If the meat is defrosted, keep it on the counter. If it is frozen and the bag or box is opened, please remember to set it on a counter.

For the shopping, at the beginning of each chapter, there is a detailed grocery list for each of the 14 meals. If you are cooking alone, simply buy what is listed. If you are working with friends, multiply the grocery list by the number of people who are coming – for example, if the list says to buy 36 chicken breasts for the month and there are 10 people cooking in your group, you will need to purchase 360 breasts. By using a food service supplier, you can get the accurate amount of chicken.

Regarding the liquid seasonings, such as soy sauce, the grocery list in each chapter lists how much you need to have to make all 14 recipes in the chapter. If you are having a group, multiply the amount by the number of people in your group to make sure you have enough spices or liquid seasonings.

With a group, normally one person is the host. If that person wants to do all the shopping for the group, that's great. If someone else wants to do the shopping, then that's also fine. The most important thing is – one person does all the shopping so you get the larger quantities and the better prices. Also, when you have one person doing the shopping, you can make sure that nothing is forgotten and you don't have to count on anyone else to bring anything to the cooking event.

When I am hosting a group for a Saturday round of cooking, I do the non-meat grocery shopping on Thursday or Friday – this includes pasta, seasonings and spices and canned items. In addition, because I shop at a food service supply location, I will buy all the onions already pre-chopped and the cheese pre-grated. Any other fresh vegetables I will have to slice up myself. I will wait until early Saturday morning to get the meat so that I can keep it frozen or at least cold in my extra refrigerator.

Because I am the host, I do all the prep work also. This includes sautéing the onions and browning the hamburger. Both of these items need to be done before everyone arrives for cooking, so the items are cooked and cooled. For the onions, I pour one or two tablespoons of oil in a large stockpot and sauté one or two large bags of precut onions in the pan; then I cool them and store in gallon freezer bags or in large covered storage containers.

Hamburger can be browned in the oven, using a jellyroll
(11 x 7) pan or a standard cake pan (9 x 13). If you don't want to use your oven, simply brown the hamburger in a large skillet, then drain and cool before everyone arrives.

If possible, buy your meat through a food service supplier so you can buy precooked, cut up chicken breasts for the casseroles. Otherwise, you will need to purchase whole chickens, boil, cool and cut up. Alternately, you can purchase pre-roasted chickens and then debone and chop up. It is easier to buy the chicken precut, instead of spending your time cutting it all up, but if you cannot use a food supplier, I would try and use the pre-roasted chickens.

When your friends arrive for cooking have them bring a cooler or a laundry basket to take their food home. If you live in a hot climate, like I do, a cooler, with a handle, for storage and transportation takes the risk out of any food borne illnesses. I do tell my friends, I have kept the food cold up till now, you are now on your own when you leave, I cannot be held responsible if you choose not to go home and immediately freeze your food. So far, I have never had a problem with anyone getting sick, but they all realize their own responsibility in taking care of their food.

Equipment needed

Many people have asked me if they need any special space or equipment to do once a month cooking. My simple answer is no and yes. Please read on for a more complete explanation.

You will be able to use standard kitchen equipment and appliances. I do recommend good quality equipment; however, you don't have to spend a lot of money on it.

If you are doing this alone, you will need two or three 2 cup measuring cups, and a one cup measuring cup, if you can find one. In addition, you will need at least 3 large bowls that hold 8 or more cups of food. We prefer the Pyrex or Pampered Chef brand bowls that have measuring levels on the outside of the bowl. A 4 cup bowl is also very handy.

I would recommend having at least 2 sets of standard measuring spoons, 4 rubber spatulas and Teflon spoons for stirring. For cutting, you will need a chef's size knife and a 5 or 6 inch knife and a couple of cutting boards.

If you are doing your cooking in a larger group of 5 or more families, you will need larger containers to mix your food in. When Vicki and I were teaching classes of 5 to 10 ladies, we used large 18 quart wash tubs to mix food in. We used gallon pitchers to mix sauces in. However, the remainder of our equipment was standard size 1 and 2 cup measuring cups, standard measuring spoons and standard pans.

An inexpensive item you will need to help your assembly go faster is either a few empty #10 cans or a couple of small plastic buckets. These cans are approximately 6 inches across and are used to put your freezer bags in. You will put the opening of the bag over the opening of the bucket or can. Then you can easily put your meat and sauce in the bag, without the bag tipping over and stuff spilling out.

There is one piece of equipment that we recommend that may not be standard for many families. You will need either an extra refrigerator in your garage to store your food in the freezer section. Another option, which tends to work better, is a free standing, upright freezer. You will find, after you start this type of cooking, that you will want to buy extra food to freeze, when it is on sale. For example, when frozen vegetables are on sale at our local stores, we stock up like crazy. Then we save time and money during the next few months of cooking and eating. Or if hamburger is on sale, we will stock up for when do the next round of cooking, or simply to have it on hand.

The containers that you will use to freeze in are inexpensive and easy to find. For any recipe that is not layered, you will use a 1 gallon freezer bag. These recipes include meat that is marinated or casseroles or soups that are meant to be stirred while cooking. Recipes that are layered, such as lasagna, will be frozen in aluminum freezer pans that have lids – these are intended to go in the freezer and the oven. All of these items are disposable when you are finished using them. If you prefer to reuse your pans, you can try to wash the aluminum pan; however, I find that they bend and don't last.

Another option for layered casseroles is an oven pan designed by Glad products. These pans come in a variety of shapes and sizes. The pan is black and the lid is clear. These are a bit pricey; however, they are intended to be used and reused. They easily go in the dishwasher for easy clean up. Also, they are intended to go in the freezer, oven and microwave. Just remember – remove the plastic lid before placing in the oven – it melts!

The last item that you will need is a set of large address labels and a pen. You will write the name of the recipe and the cooking instructions on the labels. Alternately, write the name of the recipe, such as Chicken Tortilla Soup, on the bag using a permanent marker. I would recommend writing down the page the recipe is found on in the book; then when you defrost, you will know what the item is and how to prepare it.

When we were doing the large rounds of cooking for 5-10 families, we would use a word processing program and the label template to enter the recipe name and cooking instructions. We would print out the pages of these labels and then affix them to the bags and boxes of meals for each person. The information was easily read and extremely helpful for everyone involved – especially non-cooking spouses or teenagers if they were to do the cooking!

Branching Out or choosing new recipes

After you have used my cookbook for a while, you may want to branch out and use recipes that are your family favorites or you may want to try out new or different recipes. Here are some tips for choosing recipes:

- If the recipe calls for pasta, cook al dente or don't cook it before freezing. When making something like Taco Twist casserole, al dente pasta works great. Lasagna noodles don't need to be cooked before layering, just add about 30 minutes extra time to your cooking.
- Always cook potatoes before freezing, otherwise they will turn black.
- Add fresh vegetables, for example, broccoli and celery, after freezing and defrosting, if possible. That will help them retain their crunchiness.
- Make sure you sauté onions before adding them; otherwise the entire meal will taste like onion.
- Spices change their intensity when they are frozen. So when choosing or preparing a meal, cut down the salt and increase any other spices, such as garlic. For

32

some reason, salt levels increase when you freeze and defrost. However flavors like garlic sometimes will decrease intensity when frozen and defrosted.

- If possible, marinate your meat raw and then cook after defrosting.

- It is even ok to marinate your meat while it is frozen – while it defrosts, it will tenderize and really soak in the flavor of the marinade!

- Choose items that don't require breading. The breading will soften after it has been frozen and/or while it is being defrosted and will not be as tasty. If choosing a recipe that requires breading, such as Swiss steak, see if you can make the recipe without the flour coating.

- Add water to recipes after freezing and defrosting. Water takes up unnecessary space in your freezer and freezer bags.

- Most importantly, cook as little as possible before assembling or freezing. No need to precook your roast or casserole before freezing. Just assemble and freeze; cook when you defrost. I found that if you precook a roast and then freeze and defrost, the meat will often be tough and dry when you go to serve. However, if you freeze with seasonings/marinade on it, then defrost and cook, you will have a tenderer, juicer entree. If you are making a casserole that includes cooked chicken or ground beef, make sure you cook this ahead of time, so that you don't have bloody, casserole.

How this book is set up

Each chapter in this book contains 14 recipes. There are six chicken, six beef, one pork and one vegetarian recipe. All the recipes are listed at the beginning of each chapter. After the recipe listing, you will find a complete grocery listing. This grocery list will tell you exactly what to purchase to do a round of once a month cooking for one family. If you are doing cooking with friends or a group, simply multiple the amount in the grocery list by the amount of people in the group. In the grocery list, I have taken the time to detail the amount of spices and liquid seasonings you will need so you don't have to go through the chapter and figure this out on your own, or start cooking and come up short!

After the grocery list, you will find a detailed list of how to prepare and assemble the recipes for the entire month.

Alternately, if you don't want to go through and do a month's worth of food assembly on one day, you can use the shopping list and simply put the meat in the freezer, then defrost and assemble as you are making dinner. The advantage to the once a month approach of assembly; however, is that you will save a lot of time assembling on one day since you will have all the ingredients out at one time

Month 1 Menu

Chicken
Chicken a la Sheila
King Ranch Casserole
Asian Chicken Salad
Lime-Grilled Chicken
Chicken Chili Verde
Spicy Citrus Chicken

Beef
Kids Favorite Meatloaf
Taco Twist Casserole
Jolene's Pot roast
Orange Beef
Swiss Steak
Asian Flank Steak

Vegetarian and Pork
Green Chili Quiche
Cantonese Apricot Pork

Month 2 Menu

Chicken
Korean Chicken
Apple Cranberry Wild Rice
Grilled Seasoned Chicken
Chicken and Rice in White Wine
Marinated Chicken Breasts
Salsa Chicken Skillet

Beef
Thai Beef Stir Fry
Oven Barbecued Short Ribs
Santa Fe Flank Steak
Steak Kabobs
Spicy Beef Brisket
Biscuit Beef Bake

Vegetarian and Pork
Easy Spinach Pie
Spicy Cuban Pork Chops

Month 3 Menu

Chicken
Dianne's Quick and Easy
  Chicken
Lemon Chicken
Chicken Mole
Santa Fe Chicken
Sunshine Chicken
Orange Dijon Chicken

Vegetarian and Pork
Jerk style Pork Tenderloin
Zucchini Quiche

Beef
Jen's Flank Steak
Moroccan Marinated Steak
Easy Goulash
BBQ Meatballs
Spicy Tenderloin
Smoky Barbecued Beef Brisket

Month 4 Menu

Chicken
Thai Chicken
Chicken Balsamic
Crockpot Chicken Tarragon
Chicken Tortilla Soup
Chinese Chicken Morsels
Honey Curry Chicken

Vegetarian and Pork
Carolina Crock Pot Pork
Greek Vegetarian Crockpot
  Stew

Beef
Zesty London Broil
Joes To Go
Shish Kebabs
Cilantro Lime Steak Tacos
Campfire Casserole
Asian Beef Salad

Month 5 Menu

Chicken
White Lightning Chicken Chili
Sweet and Sour Chicken

Vegetarian and Pork
Sausage Rice Skillet
Chili Rellenos Casserole
Pizza Chicken Italiano
Mandarin Orange Chicken
Indonesian Chicken Satay
Honey Lime Grilled Chicken

Beef
Ground Beef Stroganoff
Smoky Barbecued Beef Brisket
Balsamic Flank Steak
Adobo Steak
BBQ Mini Meatloaves
Jerk Beef Tenderloin

Month 6 Menu

Chicken
Grilled Mojo Chicken
Curry Chicken and Broccoli
Grilled Seasoned Chicken
Margarita Chicken
Mexican Chicken Lasagna
Chicken and Artichoke
    Casserole

Vegetarian and Pork
Easy Black Bean Chili
Apricot Glazed Pork Medallions

Beef
Port marinated Top Sirloin
Brisket with Cranberry Gravy
5 Bean Bake
Stuffed Peppers
Montreal Flank Steak
Sesame Beef Tenderloin

Month 1 Menu

Chicken
Chicken a la Sheila
King Ranch Casserole
Asian Chicken Salad
Lime-Grilled Chicken
Chicken Chili Verde
Spicy Citrus Chicken

Beef
Kids Favorite Meatloaf
Taco Twist Casserole
Jolene's Pot roast
Orange Beef
Swiss Steak
Asian Flank Steak

Vegetarian and Pork
Green Chili Quiche
Cantonese Apricot Pork

Grocery List

Meat

18 chicken breasts	2 whole chickens (can be raw or pre-roasted)
2 ½ to 3 pounds chicken pieces	3 ½ pounds ground beef (or turkey)
1 pound beef sirloin steak	2-3 pound sirloin tip roast
1 ½ pounds beef boneless round, tip or chuck steak	1 ½ to 2 pounds flank steak
1 ½ pounds pork tenderloin	

Canned items

15 oz. can whole berry cranberry sauce	1 bottle Catalina (French) dressing
1 can condensed cream of mushroom soup	1 can condensed cream of chicken soup
10 oz. can Ro*Tel diced tomatoes & green chilies	2-15 oz. cans pinto beans
15 oz. can black beans	¾ cup lime juice
8 corkscrew macaroni	15 oz. can tomato sauce
15 oz. canned corn	3-16 oz. can diced stewed tomatoes
2-4 oz. can diced green chilies	8 oz. can water chestnuts
30 oz. can apricot halves	

Refrigerated items

butter/margarine	12 corn tortillas
24 oz. shredded cheddar cheese	8 oz. grated Monterey Jack cheese
2 cups half and half	lemon juice
6 oz. can frozen pineapple-orange concentrate	1 cup sour cream
5 eggs	1 cup orange juice

Fresh fruits and vegetables

green bell pepper (optional)	2 bulbs garlic
fresh ginger	celery
2 whole onions	

Seasonings

Bread crumbs – Italian seasoned
1 package dried onion soup mix
1 package (dry) Zesty Italian salad dressing mix
1 package brown gravy mix
1 package taco seasoning

Kitchen Staples

dry ginger	ground red pepper
dry mustard	cumin
cinnamon	sesame oil
honey	cayenne pepper
$2/_3$ cup soy sauce	salt
1 cup ketchup	onion salt
apple cider vinegar	chicken bouillon
beef bouillon	½ cup olive oil
½ cup vegetable oil	garlic powder
oregano	cloves
rosemary	thyme

NB – all fresh ingredients that are needed later are not listed on the grocery list. You will want to buy these fresh as you need them.

Storage Containers Needed

13 1 gallon freezer bags
1 9 x 13 freezer to oven pan – can be plastic or aluminum. Must have a lid.

You will also need 1 or more #10 cans. You will use this can for holding your storage bag as you place the food in the bag.
#10 cans are found in the industrial size food areas in grocery stores. You can also found these cans in warehouse stores. They typically hold 6 or 7 pounds of canned food. Buy one can of something you can use, such as corn or tomatoes. After removing and using the food, wash the can and keep on hand for each month's cooking.
I normally have 2 or 3 of these cans on hand, so I can prepare more than 1 recipe at a time.
Read the chapter on Group Cooking regarding the number of cans you will need for a group setting.

Preparations needed before assembling dishes

- Boil whole chickens for King Ranch Casserole and Chicken Chili Verde. After chicken is boiled, cool and debone. Cut up in to bite size pieces. Alternately – you can purchase pre-roasted chickens at the grocery store and then remove skin and debone and cut up in to bite size pieces
- Cook pasta for Taco Twist casserole. Drain, rinse and cool
- Chop all onions and sauté until translucent. Use ¼ cup butter per onion.
- If using, sauté green bell pepper for King Ranch Casserole
- Brown ground beef for Taco Twist. Drain and cool
- If desired, slice pork into strips for Cantonese Apricot Pork. This recipe works fine if the pork is not sliced before cooking.
- Before assembling meals, label all bags with the name of the recipe. Use a permanent marker.
- Assemble meals in whichever order you choose.
- Promptly freeze meals to avoid any potential illness.

Chicken a la Sheila

6 boneless skinless chicken breasts – thighs also work well
15 ¾ oz. can of whole berry cranberry sauce
1 package dried onion soup mix
1 bottle Catalina dressing (also called French dressing)

1. Place 1 gallon bag in #10 can
2. Place chicken breasts in 1 gallon freezer bag.
3. In a medium bowl, mix cranberry sauce, onion soup mix and Catalina dressing
4. Pour mixture over chicken and freeze.

To prepare: Defrost mixture. Preheat oven to 350F. Place chicken and sauce in 9 x 13 pan, cover container with foil and place in oven. Bake for 1 hour. Remove foil and continue baking for 15 minutes.
Alternately, pour entire bag into crock pot and cook on low 6-8 hours.

Serve with brown rice and steamed green beans

Serves: 6

King Ranch Casserole

¼ cup butter or margarine
1 medium green bell pepper, chopped (this is optional)
1 medium onion, chopped
2 cups cubed cooked chicken (see note)
1 can (10 ¾ oz.) condensed cream of mushroom soup
1 can (10 ¾ oz.) condensed cream of chicken soup
1 can (10 oz.) RO*TEL Diced Tomatoes & Green Chilies
12 corn tortillas, torn into bite-sized pieces
2 cups (8 oz.) shredded cheddar cheese

*If you followed the instructions at the beginning of this chapter, the bell pepper and onion will already be sautéed and the chicken will be cooked and cut up, then start with step 3. If not, please start at the beginning of this recipe.

1. In a large saucepan, cook pepper and onion in butter or margarine until tender, about 5 minutes. Cool completely before going to step 3
2. Cook chicken. Cool and cut up.
3. Add soups, RO*TEL and chicken, stirring until well blended.
4. Spray 9 x 13 baking pan with oil.
5. Layer ingredients starting with a light layer of soup, then tortillas, soup and cheese. Repeat layering for three layers. Cover pan with foil or lid and freeze.

To prepare: Defrost mixture in fridge. Preheat oven to 325F. Bake until bubbly, approximately 30 minutes. Remove foil and bake for an additional 15 minutes.

Serve with Spanish rice and a green salad.

Serves: 8.

Note: 1 boiled or pre-roasted chicken will give you 3 cups chopped chicken. This recipe can use up to 3 cups of chicken, if desired.

Asian Chicken Salad

½ cup olive oil
2 TBSP apple cider vinegar
2-4 TBSP soy sauce
4 TSP dark sesame oil
2 TSP honey
1 garlic clove, minced
½ TSP minced fresh ginger
2 TSP salt (sea salt if possible)
6 boneless skinless chicken breasts

Ingredients needed later/Optional ingredients
2 TBSP sesame seeds, toasted
Chopped romaine lettuce, or mixed salad greens
Asparagus spears
Red bell pepper, chopped
Sugar snap peas
1 can sliced water chestnuts, drained

1. In large bowl or pitcher, mix all ingredients, except chicken breasts, until well combined.
2. Place 1 gallon freezer bag in #10 can
3. Add chicken and marinade (approximately $^2/_3$ cup per person, add more if there is some left over).
4. Seal bag and shake to combine. Freeze.

To prepare: Defrost mixture. Remove chicken from marinade, place marinade in large sauce pan and cook until boiling; cool. Cook chicken on the stove or barbecue until done and no longer pink.
If desired, cut chicken up. Place on salad greens, add additional toppings. Use cooked marinade for dressing.

Serves: 6

Lime-Grilled Chicken

6 boneless skinless chicken breasts
¾ cup lime juice
$1/3$ cup vegetable oil
3 TBSP honey
1 ½ TSP thyme
1 ½ TSP rosemary
2 garlic cloves, crushed

1. Place 1 gallon freezer bag in #10 can
2. Place chicken in bag
3. Place all remaining ingredients in bag.
4. Seal bag and shake to combine. Freeze

To prepare: Defrost mixture. Remove chicken from bag, discard marinade. Barbecue chicken until done.

Serve with quinoa and steamed asparagus.

Serves: 6

Chicken Chili Verde

¾ cup finely chopped onion, sautéed
1 TSP vegetable oil
3 cups cooked chicken, chopped
2 15 oz. cans pinto beans, drain 1 can, do not drain other
1-4 oz. can chopped green chilies (more if you like spicier food)
2-15 oz. cans chopped tomatoes (use Mexican style if desired)
1 TSP ground cumin
1 TSP dried oregano leaves
$^1/_8$ TSP ground cloves
¼ TSP cayenne pepper
1 TBSP chicken bouillon
2 cloves minced garlic
1 TSP salt

*If you followed the instructions at the beginning of this chapter, the onion will already be sautéed and the chicken will be cooked, then start with step 3. If not, please start at the beginning of this recipe.

1. Sauté onion in 1 TSP vegetable oil
2. Boil chicken, cool completely, debone and chop
3. Place 1 gallon freezer bag in #10 can.
4. Place all ingredients in 1 gallon freezer bag. Seal bag and shake to combine. Freeze.

To prepare: Defrost mixture. Place mixture in large sauce pan; add 3 cups water. Heat soup until boiling.

Serve with quesadillas and salsa, if desired.

Serves: 6

Note: 1 boiled or pre-roasted chicken will give you 3 cups chopped chicken. This recipe can use up to 3 cups of chicken, if desired.

Spicy Citrus Chicken

6 oz. can frozen pineapple-orange concentrate, thawed
   (approx. ¾ cup)
½ cup ketchup
2 TBSP lemon juice
¼ TSP ground red pepper (or more to taste)
2 ½ to 3 pounds chicken pieces

Ingredients needed later
2 TBSP quick-cooking tapioca
1 stick cinnamon
8 whole allspice
4 whole cloves
1 piece cheese cloth and string

1. Place first 4 ingredients in bowl and mix well.
2. Place 1 gallon freezer bag in #10 can
3. Add chicken and sauce
4. Seal bag and shake; freeze

To prepare: Defrost mixture. Place tapioca in bottom of crockpot. Add chicken and marinade. In a piece of cheese cloth, place cinnamon, allspice and cloves. Tie closed with string and place on top of chicken.
Cover and cook on low heat for 8-10 hours or high heat for 4-5 hours. When chicken is done, remove and discard seasoning bag. Remove chicken to serving platter. Thicken sauce, if desired.

Serve chicken with hot rice and steamed Asian vegetables.

Serves: 6-8

Kids' Favorite Meatloaf/ Meatballs

2 eggs
2 pounds ground beef
¾ cup bread crumbs – use Italian seasoned
½ cup ketchup, chili sauce or barbecue sauce
1 TSP onion salt
1 TSP salt
1 TSP garlic powder

1. Mix all ingredients together in a large bowl.
2. Place 1 gallon freezer bag in #10 can.
3. Place mixture in 1 gallon freezer bag and freeze.

To prepare: Defrost mixture. Preheat oven to 350F. Remove mixture from bag and place in loaf pan or round cake pan. If baking in a loaf pan, bake for 1 hour. If baking in a round cake pan, bake for 25-30 minutes.
In last 10 minutes, squeeze extra ketchup, barbecue sauce or chili sauce on top of cooking meat. When the meat is done, let stand for 10 minutes before slicing.

Meatball option: Shape mixture into 1 inch meatballs. Bake at 400 in a 9 x 13 x 2 pan for 20 minutes.

Serve with garlic mashed potatoes and green salad

Serves: 6-8

Taco Twist Casserole

3 cups corkscrew macaroni (8 oz.) -- cooked and drained (gluten free pasta works in this)
1 ½ pounds hamburger, browned and drained (turkey can be substituted)
1 package taco seasoning mix
15 oz. can tomato sauce
15 oz. can of black beans, drained and rinsed
15 oz. can corn, drained
2 cups cheese – shredded (8 oz.) (Cheddar or Monterey Jack is fine)
1 cup sour cream

*If you followed the instructions at the beginning of this chapter, the pasta will already be cooked and the hamburger will already be browned, then start with step 3. If not, please start at the beginning of this recipe.

1. Cook pasta until al dente, drain and set aside.
2. Brown ground beef, drain and cool.
3. In a large bowl mix all ingredients, including pasta and hamburger.
4. Place 1 gallon freezer bag in #10 can
5. Pour entire mix into 1 gallon freezer bag, seal and freeze.

To prepare: Defrost mixture. Preheat oven to 350. Pour mixture in greased or sprayed 9 x 9 or 8 x 8 pan. Cover with foil and bake for 20 minutes. Remove foil, bake for an additional 10 minutes or until thoroughly heated.

Serve with steamed broccoli or spinach salad

Serves: 6-8

Jolene's Pot Roast

2-3 pounds sirloin tip roast
1 pkg. Zesty Italian salad dressing mix
1 pkg. Brown gravy mix
2 TSP beef bouillon

Ingredients Needed Later
3 cups water
¼ cup water
3 TBSP cornstarch

1. Place 1 gallon freezer bag in #10 can
2. Place all ingredients in bag.
3. Massage dry ingredients in to meat. Seal bag and freeze.

To prepare: Defrost mixture. Place mixture in crockpot; add 3 cups water. Cook on low 8-10 hours or on high 4-6 hours. The longer and slower you cook this, the better it tastes.

Before serving, remove meat and shred. Put sauce in large sauce pan. In small bowl, mix remaining water and cornstarch until cornstarch is incorporated. Add to sauce and boil until thickened and gravy-like.

Serve with mashed potatoes or on hard rolls.

Serves: 6-8

Orange Beef

1 pound beef sirloin steak
2 TBSP soy sauce
½ TSP ground ginger
½ TSP garlic powder
1 cup orange juice

Ingredients Needed Later
3 TBSP vegetable oil
½ cup cold water
2 TBSP cornstarch
1 pound bag frozen stir fry vegetables

1. Trim fat from beef steak. Cut beef with grain into 2 inch strips. Cut strips across grain into $1/_8$ inch slices.
2. Place 1 gallon freezer bag in #10 can
3. Place all ingredients in 1 gallon freezer bag. Seal and shake to combine. Freeze.

To prepare: Defrost mixture. Heat wok or 12-inch skillet until hot. Add 3 TBSP oil and rotate pan to coat sides. Add beef, reserving marinade. Stir-fry about 3 minutes or until beef is brown. Meanwhile, heat frozen stir fry vegetables.
In separate bowl, mix marinade, water and cornstarch. When beef is cooked, add marinade, cook and stir about 1 minute or until thickened.
Add stir-fry vegetables and heat until bubbly.

Serve over steamed rice with stir fry vegetables.

Serves: 6-8

Asian Flank Steak Marinade

1 ½ to 2 pounds flank steak
¼ cup soy sauce
3 TSBP honey
$^1/_3$ cup oil
½ TSP ground ginger
1 clove garlic - pressed

1. Place 1 gallon freezer bag in #10 can
2. Place flank steak in 1 gallon freezer bag.
3. Mix other items together in a small bowl and pour over steak and freeze.

To prepare: Defrost steak. Preheat oven to broil, or heat grill to 400F. Remove steak from bag and discard marinade. Place steak on grill or on broiler pan and cook for 7-10 minutes on one side, turn over and cook until desired doneness is achieved.

Serve with baked potatoes and steamed broccoli

Serves: 6-8

Swiss Steak

1 ½ pounds beef boneless round, tip or chuck steak, about ¾ inch thick
1 TSP dry mustard
½ TSP salt
2 TBSP vegetable oil
16 oz. can diced stewed tomatoes
2 cloves garlic, finely chopped

Ingredients Needed Later
1 cup water
1 large onion, sliced
1 large green bell pepper, sliced - optional

1. Place 1 gallon freezer bag in #10 can
2. Cut steak in to 6 serving pieces.
3. Place all ingredients in bag. Seal bag, shake to combine and freeze.

To prepare: Defrost mixture. Place in large covered fry pan. Cover and simmer about 1 ¼ hours or until beef is tender. Add water, onion and bell pepper. Heat to boiling; reduce heat. Cover and simmer 5-8 minutes or until vegetables are tender. Alternately, Defrost mixture, place in crock pot. Cook on low 8-10 hours or on high for 4-6 hours.

Serve over cooked pasta or steamed rice.

Serves: 6-8

Green Chile Quiche

3 lightly beaten eggs
1 ¼ cups grated Monterey Jack cheese
¾ cup Grated mild cheddar
4 oz. can diced green chilies
1 cup half and half (see note)
½ TSP salt
$1/_8$ TSP ground cumin
$1/_8$ TSP ground cinnamon

Ingredients Needed Later
9 inch deep dish frozen pie shell

1. Place 1 gallon freezer bag in #10 can
2. In a small bowl, beat eggs.
3. Pour all ingredients in freezer bag. Seal bag and shake to combine. Place in freezer.

To prepare: Defrost mixture. Pour into pie shell. Bake uncovered in 325F oven for 40 to 50 minutes.

Serve with quesadillas (cheese melted on flour tortillas)

Serves: 6-8

Note: If you desire a lower fat quiche, 1 cup whole milk or ½ cup whole and ½ cup 2% milk may be substituted.

Cantonese Apricot Pork

2 TBSP vegetable oil
½ cup sliced onion, sautéed
1 ½ pounds pork tenderloin – sliced into thin strips
2 cups sliced celery
2 cloves garlic, minced
$1/_3$ cup soy sauce
¾ TSP powdered ginger
8 oz. can water chestnuts – drained
30 oz. can apricot halves, drained

Ingredients Needed Later
3 TBSP cornstarch
¼ cup water

*If you followed the instructions at the beginning of this chapter, the onion will already be sautéed and the pork will be sliced into strips, then start with step 3. If not, please start at the beginning of this recipe.

1. Sauté onion in vegetable oil. Cool completely before going on to step 3.
2. Cut pork tenderloin into thin strips
3. Place 1 gallon bag in #10 can.
4. Pour all ingredients in to bag. Shake to combine and freeze.

To prepare: Defrost mixture. Heat large covered fry pan. Add meat and cook until pork is cooked through. Add sauce and cook until boiled and slightly thickened. If desired, mix 3 TBSP cornstarch with ¼ cup water and add to sauce to thicken it. If you prefer, you can cook in a slower cooker, on low, for 6-8 hours.

Serve over rice.

Serves: 6

Month 2 Menu

Chicken
Korean Chicken
Apple Cranberry Wild Rice
Grilled Seasoned Chicken
Chicken and Rice in White Wine
Marinated Chicken Breasts
Salsa Chicken Skillet

Beef
Thai Beef Stir Fry
Oven Barbecued Short Ribs
Santa Fe Flank Steak
Steak Kabobs
Spicy Beef Brisket
Biscuit Beef Bake

Vegetarian and Pork
Easy Spinach Pie
Spicy Cuban Pork Chops

Grocery List

Meat

1 whole chicken raw or pre-roasted	30 chicken breasts
4-5 pounds beef short ribs	1 pound ground beef
3 ½ pounds beef sirloin steaks	2 pounds flank steak
3-4 pounds beef brisket	6 thick pork chops

Canned Items

Pancake and biscuit mix	1 box instant Wild rice & seasoning mix
Dried cranberries	Dried apples
Lemon juice	½ cup Lime juice
2 cups lemon lime soda	2 cups chunky salsa
Red currant jelly	2 4 oz. cans chopped green chilies
¼ cup Italian Salad dressing (prepared)	1 cup Chili sauce (spicy ketchup)
8 oz. can tomato sauce	½ cup canned corn
14 ½ oz. can Mexican-style stewed tomatoes	15 oz. can black beans

Refrigerated Items

6 TBSP Butter	1 cup orange juice
16 oz. cottage cheese	½ cup grated parmesan cheese
4 eggs	¼ cup milk
10 oz. frozen chopped spinach	4 oz. Monterey jack cheese, shredded

Vegetables

5 whole onions	½ cup dried cranberries
½ cup dried apples	1 leek
2 bulbs garlic	Bunch cilantro
1 jalapeno pepper	

Seasonings

prepared horseradish (not creamy)	savory
lemon pepper seasoning	balsamic vinegar
4 cups White wine	

Kitchen Staples

chicken bouillon	cumin
salt	Black pepper
onion salt	$2/3$ cup olive oil
$1/3$ cup Worcestershire sauce	1 $2/3$ cup soy sauce
garlic powder	1 ¼ cup brown sugar
cornstarch	beef bouillon
onion powder	dry ginger
hot sauce (such as Tabasco)	peanut butter
seasoned salt	oregano
$2/3$ cup vegetable oil	1 cup ketchup
marjoram	basil
rosemary	chili powder
$1/3$ cup cider vinegar	cinnamon
celery seed	½ cup white vinegar
dry parsley	dried onion
bay leaves	$1/3$ cup red wine vinegar

NB – all fresh ingredients that are needed later are not listed on the grocery list. You will want to buy these fresh as you need them.

Storage containers needed

13 1 gallon freezer bags
1 9 x 13 freezer to oven safe pan – can be aluminum or plastic. Must have a lid.

You will also need 1 or more #10 cans. You will use this can for holding your storage bag as you place the food in the bag.
#10 cans are found in the industrial size food areas in grocery stores. You can also find these cans in warehouse stores. They typically hold 6 or 7 pounds of canned food. Buy one can of something you can use, after removing and using the food, wash the can and keep on hand for each month's cooking.
I normally have 2 or 3 of these cans on hand, so I can prepare more than 1 recipe at a time.

Preparations needed before assembling dishes

1. Boil chicken or buy a pre-roasted chicken for Apple Cranberry Wild Rice. After chicken is cooked, cool and debone. Cut up meat in to bite size pieces.
2. Chop onions and sauté for Spicy Beef Brisket and Easy Spinach Pie. Use olive oil or vegetable oil
3. Cook wild rice according to box instructions.
4. Slice meat for Thai Beef and Steak Kabobs
5. Before assembling meals, label all bags with the name of the recipe. Use a permanent marker.
6. Assemble meals in whichever order you choose.
7. Promptly freeze meals to avoid any potential illness.

Korean Chicken

6 boneless skinless chicken breasts
¼ cup soy sauce
2 TBSP vegetable oil
2 TBSP sherry or white wine
½ TSP ground ginger
½ TSP cinnamon
2 garlic cloves, finely chopped

1. Place 1 gallon freezer bag in #10 can
2. Place all chicken in bag
3. Pour marinade over chicken
4. Seal bag and shake to combine; freeze

To prepare: Defrost mixture. Remove chicken from marinade and discard marinade. Cook chicken on barbecue until finished.

Serve with rice or cut up and serve on salad

Serves: 6

Apple Cranberry Wild Rice

1 cup dry wild rice (cooked according to package instructions)
3 cups cut-up cooked chicken (see note)
1 TSP dried savory
¼ TSP onion salt
½ TSP lemon pepper seasoning
1 small (white portion only) leek, coarsely chopped
1 TSP olive oil
½ cup dried cranberries
½ cup chopped dried apples
6 TBSP chicken broth (mix ½ cup water with ½ TSP chicken
   bouillon)

*If you followed the instructions at the beginning of this chapter, the rice will be prepared and the chicken will be cooked, cooled and cut up, then start with step 3. If not, please start at the beginning of this recipe.

1. Cook rice, according to package instructions. Cool.
2. Cook chicken. Cool and cut up
3. Place 1 gallon freezer bag in #10 can.
4. Add all ingredients, seal and shake to combine; freeze.

To prepare: Defrost mixture, heat and simmer for 6-8 minutes or until fruit is tender.

Serve with cooked butternut squash.

Serves: 6-8

Note: 1 boiled or pre-roasted chicken will give you 3 cups chopped chicken. This recipe can use up to 3 cups of chicken, if desired.

Grilled Seasoned Chicken

6 boneless skinless chicken breasts
¼ cup prepared Italian salad dressing
2 TBSP lemon juice
2 TBSP balsamic vinegar
2 TBSP olive oil
3 garlic cloves

1. Place 1 gallon freezer bag in #10 can.
2. Add all ingredients to bag, seal and shake to combine; freeze.

To prepare: Defrost mixture. Preheat grill or oven. Remove chicken from marinade and discard marinade. Cook on grill 10 minutes, turn and cook additional 5 minutes or until juices run clear.

If desired, boil marinade and then brush on chicken as it cooks.

Serve with green salad and steamed pasta tossed with butter and garlic

Serves: 6

Chicken and Rice in White Wine

6 boneless skinless chicken breasts
4 cups white wine
6 TBSP melted butter
2 TBSP dried parsley
2 TBSP dried onion
1 TSP garlic powder
½ TSP seasoned salt

Ingredients needed later
2 cups uncooked rice

1. Place 1 gallon bag in #10 can
2. Place chicken in bag
3. Pour remaining ingredients over chicken
4. Seal bag. Shake to combine. Freeze

To prepare: Defrost mixture. Preheat oven to 450 degrees. Place chicken and marinade in 9 x 13 pan. Bake for 35 minutes. Turn the chicken over. Add the rice and more wine if necessary. Continue cooking 20 minutes longer or until the rice is tender.

Optionally – cook the chicken and wine separately. Serve chicken on top of wine and pour sauce over the top. If you do not like or use wine, apple juice can be used instead. It will give the chicken a sweeter flavor, but is still delicious!

Serves: 6

Marinated Chicken Breasts

6 boneless skinless chicken breast halves
2 cups lemon-lime soda
1 cup soy sauce
½ cup olive oil
½ TSP garlic powder
½ TSP prepared horseradish

1. Place 1 gallon freezer bag in #10 can.
2. Add all ingredients, seal and shake to combine; freeze.

To prepare: Defrost mixture. Drain chicken. If desired, place marinade in large sauce pan and cook until bubbly. Grill chicken, uncovered, over medium heat for 6-7 minutes on each side or until juice run clear. Spoon marinade over chicken.

Serve with boiled potatoes with green beans and dill.

Serves: 6

Salsa Chicken Skillet

6 boneless, skinless chicken breasts
2 cups chunky salsa

Ingredients needed later
2 TBSP oil, divided
½ pound fresh mushrooms, sliced
1 medium green pepper, chopped
¾ cup chopped onion
½ cup chopped celery
½ cup frozen corn, thawed
1 garlic clove, minced

Optional Ingredients
Shredded Cheese
Sour Cream

1. Place 1 gallon freezer bag in #10 can.
2. Add all ingredients, seal and shake to combine; freeze.

To prepare: Defrost mixture. Heat 1 TBSP oil in large pan. Add chicken and salsa, cook until chicken is done. Remove chicken and salsa from pan and allow to rest. Heat remaining oil and sauté mushrooms, green pepper, onion, celery corn and garlic for 6-8 minutes or until vegetables are crisp tender.

Serve each chicken breast with some salsa and vegetables over Spanish rice. Top with cheese and sour cream if desired.

Serves: 6

Thai Beef Stir-Fry

2 pounds boneless beef sirloin steak, cut into strips.
½ cup packed brown sugar
2 TBSP cornstarch
2 TSP beef bouillon
$\frac{1}{3}$ cup soy sauce
1 TSP onion powder
1 TSP ground ginger
¼ TSP hot pepper sauce (or more to taste)
¼ cup peanut butter

Ingredients needed later
4 TBSP oil – can be vegetable, olive or peanut
1 ½ cups julienned carrots
4 cups fresh broccoli florets
2 cups sliced fresh mushrooms
2 cups water

If you followed the instructions at the beginning of the chapter, the meat will already be cut up, start at step 2. If you did not follow those instructions, start with step 1.

1. Cut meat in to strips for stir fry.
2. Place 1 gallon freezer bag in #10 can.
3. Add beef to bag.
4. In separate bowl, combine remaining ingredients and stir till well combined; pour over meat. Seal bag and shake to combine; freeze.

To prepare: Defrost mixture. In a large skillet or wok heat 3 TBSP oil. Remove meat from bag, reserving marinade. Place meat mixture in pan, stir fry until meat is done. Add carrots and cook for 5 minutes. Add broccoli; stir-fry for 7 minutes. Add mushrooms; stir-fry 6-8 minutes longer or until vegetables are crisp-tender. In a stock pot, combine marinade plus 2 cups water, bring to a boil; cook and stir for 2 minutes or until thickened.

Serve over steamed rice or cooked spaghetti. Top with chopped peanuts if desired.   Serves: 6-8

Oven Barbecued Short Ribs

4-5 pounds beef short ribs (lean)
1 very large onion, finely chopped and sautéed
1 TSP celery seeds
1 TSP salt
¼ cup vinegar
¼ cup Worcestershire sauce
1 cup ketchup
¼ cup brown sugar

Ingredients needed later
2 cups water

1. Place 1 gallon freezer bag in #10 can
2. Place beef ribs in bag
3. Seal bag.
4. In 2nd bag, place remaining ingredients. Seal bag and shake to combine.
5. Freeze both bags

To prepare: Defrost both bags. Preheat oven to 350. Place meat fat side down in shallow roasting pan and salt lightly. Bake uncovered for 35-40 minutes. Drain off any fat. In a large saucepan, combine the remaining ingredients and bring to a boil. Pour the hot sauce over the meat. Reduce the oven temperature to 300 degrees and cook for 1 ½ to 2 hours, or until done. Baste frequently.

Serve with quinoa or wild rice and steamed mixed vegetables.

Serves: 6-8

Santa Fe Flank Steak

½ cup chopped onion
1 TBSP olive oil
2 cans (4 oz. each) chopped green chilies
½ cup fresh cilantro leaves
1 jalapeno pepper, seeded
2 TSP red currant jelly
1 TSP chicken bouillon granules
1 TSP Worcestershire sauce
½ TSP seasoned salt
¼ TSP dried oregano
1 ½ to 2 pounds flank steak

Ingredients Needed Later
½ cup shredded Monterey Jack cheese

If you followed the instructions at the beginning of the chapter, the onion will already be cooked, start at step 2. If you did not follow those instructions, start with step 1.

1. In a small saucepan, sauté onion in oil until tender. Cool completely.
2. Place all ingredients, except steak, in blender. Cover and process until smooth.
3. Place 1 gallon freezer bag in #10 can. Add all ingredients, seal and shake to combine; freeze.

To prepare: Defrost mixture. Place marinade in large sauce pan and heat until boiling. Grill steaks until desired doneness is achieved. Serve steak with green chili sauce and sprinkle with cheese, if desired.

Serve with Spanish rice and black beans

Serves: 6

Steak Kabobs

1 ½ pounds boneless beef sirloin steak
½ cup vegetable oil
$1/3$ cup red wine vinegar
2 TBSP Ketchup
2 to 3 garlic cloves, minced
1 TSP Worcestershire sauce
½ TSP each dried marjoram, basil and oregano
½ TSP dried rosemary, crushed

Ingredients Needed Later
1 ½ cups cherry tomatoes
½ pound whole fresh mushrooms
2 medium onions cut into wedges
2 small green peppers cut into 1 inch pieces

If you followed the instructions at the beginning of the chapter, the steak will already be cut up, start at step 2. If you did not follow those instructions, start with step 1.

1. Cut steak into 1-inch cubes and place in 1 gallon freezer bag.
2. Place 1 gallon freezer bag in #10 can.
3. Add remaining ingredients over steak. Seal bag, shake to combine; freeze.

To prepare: Defrost mixture. Drain meat. If desired, place marinade in large sauce pan and heat until bubbly. Cut up desired vegetables and alternately thread beef and vegetables onto six metal or soaked wooden skewers. Grill covered 6-8 minutes. While grilling, brush meat and vegetables with cooked marinade. Turn kabobs and cook 4-6 minutes longer or until beef reaches desired doneness.

Serve with steamed wild rice mixture.

Serves: 6

Spicy Beef Brisket

2 TBSP olive oil
2 large onions, sliced
1 fresh beef brisket (approximately 3 pounds)
½ TSP seasoned salt
¼ TSP pepper
3 garlic cloves, minced
1 TSP beef bouillon
1 cup chili sauce
$1/3$ cup packed brown sugar
$1/3$ cup cider vinegar
2-3 TBSP chili powder
2 bay leaves

Ingredients needed Later
3 TBSP all-purpose flour
1 ¼ cup cold water

If you followed the instructions at the beginning of the chapter, the onions will already be sautéed, start at step 2. If you did not follow those instructions, start with step 1.

1. Sauté onions in olive oil. Cool completely.
2. Place 1 gallon freezer bag in #10 can.
3. Add all ingredients, seal and shake to combine; freeze.

To prepare; Defrost mixture. Place contents of bag in crock pot. Cook on low 8-10 hours or on high 4-6 hours. When meat is done, remove from crock pot and allow to rest for 5-10 minutes. Mix flour and water in a cup, then add to sauce in crock pot and cook until sauce is slightly thickened.

Serve with mashed potatoes and sauce.

Serves: 6-8

Biscuit Beef Bake

1 pound lean ground beef (2 cups cooked)
½ cup onion, chopped and sautéed
1 garlic clove, minced
1 14 ½ oz. can Mexican-style stewed tomatoes, undrained
1 15 oz. can black beans, rinsed and drained
1 8 oz. can tomato sauce
½ cup corn
2 TSP chili powder
1 TSP cumin
1 TSP salt

Ingredients needed later
1 12 oz. package Hungry Jack buttermilk biscuits

*If you followed the instructions at the beginning of this chapter, the ground beef and onion will already be sautéed, then start with step 2. If not, please start at the beginning of this recipe.

1. Cook ground beef and onion until beef is no longer pink and onion is translucent; cool.
2. Place 1 gallon freezer bag in #10 can.
3. Combine all ingredients in bag.
4. Seal bag and freeze.

To prepare: Defrost mixture. Heat in large fry pan for 15 minutes. Serve on top of biscuits.
Alternately, heat oven to 400F. Transfer mixture to greased or sprayed 8 x 8 ovenproof dish. Arrange the biscuits on top and bake for 15-20 minutes, or until done.

Serve with green salad

Serves: 6

Easy Spinach Pie

1 cup prepared pancake and biscuit mix
¼ cup milk
2 eggs
¼ cup finely chopped onion
1 10 oz. package frozen chopped spinach, thawed and drained
½ cup grated Parmesan cheese
4 oz. Monterey Jack cheese, shredded
1 16 oz. carton cottage cheese
½ TSP salt
2 cloves garlic, crushed
2 eggs

1. Grease 9 x 13 oven-proof pan.
2. Mix pancake and biscuit mix, milk, 2 eggs and onion; beat vigorously 20 strokes. Spread in dish.
3. Mix remaining ingredients; spoon evenly over batter in pan. Cover and freeze.

To prepare: Defrost mixture. Preheat oven to 350F. Remove plastic lid on pan, if it is covered with one. Cover pan with foil and bake for 20 minutes. Remove from oven, remove oil and return to oven for an additional 10 minutes, or until pie is set.

Serve with cooked pasta tossed with butter and garlic

Serves: 6-8

Spicy Cuban Pork Chops

6 large, bone in pork chops
1 cup orange juice
½ cup lime juice
¼ cup white vinegar
2 TBSP vegetable oil
1 TBSP black pepper
1 TBSP salt
1 ½ TSBP ground cumin
1 TSBP chili powder
1 TBSP garlic powder
1 TBSP onion powder
1 TBSP dried oregano

1. Place 1 gallon freezer bag in #10 can.
2. Add all liquid ingredients, seal and shake to combine; freeze.
3. Mix all dry seasonings in a small sealable sandwich bag and freeze with pork chops.

To prepare: Defrost mixture. Mix pepper, salt, cumin, chili powder, garlic powder, onion powder and oregano in a small bowl. Remove pork chops from bag and reserve marinade. Dry off pork chops and coat both sides with dry spice mixture. Add oil to large pan, heat over high heat. When oil is hot, add pork chops. Cook on first side until brown, about 3-5 minutes. Turn pork chops over, turn heat down to medium high. Cook 3-5 minutes longer and then add half of marinade, discard remaining marinade. Cook about 5 minutes longer or until sauce is reduced by half and starts to thicken. Remove pork chops, allow to rest for 5 minutes so juices redistribute. Cook marinade another 5 minutes until well reduced and thickened.

Serve pork chops with sauce spooned on top. Serve with garlic mashed potatoes and green salad

Serves: 6

Month 3 Menu

Chicken
Dianne's Quick and Easy Chicken
Lemon Chicken
Chicken Mole
Santa Fe Chicken
Sunshine Chicken
Orange Dijon Chicken

Beef
Jen's Flank Steak
Moroccan Marinated Steak
Easy Goulash
BBQ Meatballs
Spicy Tenderloin
Smoky Barbecued Beef Brisket

Vegetarian and Pork
Jerk style Pork Tenderloin
Zucchini Quiche

Grocery List

Meat

36 chicken breasts	12 slices lean bacon
1 ⅓ – 2 pounds flank steak	2-3 pounds beef tenderloin
2 ½ pounds ground beef	2-3 pounds pork tenderloins
1 ½ pounds London broil	2-3 pound beef brisket

Canned Items

1 cup prepared Italian dressing	4 cans golden mushroom soup
½ cup tomato sauce	¼ cup bread crumbs
1 square unsweetened chocolate	3 TBSP lime juice
1 cup lemon juice	1 can cream of chicken soup
1 ¼ cup pineapple juice	¾ cup orange juice
2 14 oz. can stewed tomatoes	8 oz. can sliced mushrooms
¾ cup pancake and waffle mix	

Refrigerated Items

8 oz. shredded mozzarella cheese	4 eggs
1 ⅔ cup milk	¼ cup sour cream

Vegetables

3 whole onions	3 bulbs garlic
fresh sage(dry works too)	1 tomato
green bell pepper	2 cups sliced zucchini

Seasonings

teriyaki sauce	lemon pepper seasoning
¼ cup red wine vinegar	½ cup Worcestershire sauce
coriander leaves	Cavender's Seasoning
¼ cup Dijon mustard	½ cup steak sauce
⅓ cup Port wine	2 TBSP red cooking wine
½ cup chili sauce	1 ½ TSP liquid smoke

Kitchen Staples

salt	honey
garlic powder	black pepper
paprika	vegetable oil
chicken bouillon	¼ cup chili powder
sugar	cinnamon
cloves	¾ cup soy sauce
olive oil	ground coriander
½ cup prepared yellow mustard	¼ cup peanut butter
dry mustard	1 $\frac{1}{3}$ cup brown sugar
ground ginger	seasoned salt
1 ¼ cup ketchup	cumin seeds
tarragon	ground cumin
white vinegar	6 TBSP dry minced onion
celery seed	Tabasco sauce
Italian seasoning	½ cup rolled oats

NB – all fresh ingredients that are needed later are not listed on the grocery list. You will want to buy these fresh as you need them.

Storage Containers Needed

13 1 gallon freezer bags
1 8 x 8 freezer to oven pan – can be plastic or aluminum. Must have a lid.

You will also need 1 or more #10 cans. You will use this can for holding your storage bag as you place the food in the bag.
#10 cans are found in the industrial size food areas in grocery stores. You can also find these cans in warehouse stores. They typically hold 6 or 7 pounds of canned food. Buy one can of something you can use, after removing and using the food, wash the can and keep on hand for each month's cooking.
I normally have 2 or 3 of these cans on hand, so I can prepare more than 1 recipe at a time.

Preparations needed before assembling dishes

- Sauté ground beef for Easy Goulash.
- Chop and sauté onions in olive or vegetable oil.
- Before assembling meals, label all bags with the name of the recipe. Use a permanent marker.
- Assemble meals in whichever order you choose.
- Promptly freeze meals to avoid any potential illness.

Dianne's Quick and Easy Chicken

6 boneless skinless chicken breasts
1 cup Italian dressing
3 TBSP teriyaki sauce
1 TSP salt
3 TBSP honey
½ TSP black pepper
2 TSP garlic minced

1. Place 1 gallon freezer bag in #10 can.
2. Place chicken in bag.
3. Pour all ingredients over chicken. Seal bag, shake to combine and freeze.

To prepare: Defrost mixture. Remove chicken from marinade; discard marinade. Grill until done.

Serve with steamed potatoes and broccoli.

Serves: 6

Lemon Chicken

6 boneless skinless chicken breasts
4 cans golden mushroom soup
2 TSP paprika
½ TSP salt
½ TSP lemon pepper
¾ TSP tarragon, crushed between fingers
6 TBSP lemon juice

1. Place 1 gallon freezer bag in 1 #10 can.
2. Place chicken in bag.
3. Combine all other ingredients in a small bowl. Pour all other ingredients over chicken.
4. Seal bag, shake to combine. Freeze.

To prepare: Defrost mixture. Place entire mixture in crock pot and cook on high 4-6 hours or on low for 8 to 10 hours.

Serve over rice

Serves: 6

Chicken Mole

1 cup onion, chopped and sautéed
6 boneless skinless chicken breasts
2 TSP salt
2 TBSP vegetable oil
2 cups chicken broth
½ cup tomato sauce
¼ cup creamy peanut butter
1 1 oz. square unsweetened chocolate, finely chopped or grated
¼ cup dry bread crumbs
¼ cup chili powder
1 ½ TSP sugar
¼ TSP ground cinnamon
¼ TSP ground cumin
¼ TSP cloves
1 garlic clove, crushed

If you followed the instructions at the beginning of the chapter, the onion will already be sautéed, start at step 2. If you did not follow those instructions, start with step 1.

1. Sauté onion. Cool completely before continuing to step 2
2. Place 1 gallon freezer bags in #10 cans.
3. Place chicken in bags.
4. Place all other items in blender and blend until well combined.
5. Pour evenly over chicken. Seal bag, shake to combine and freeze.

To prepare: Defrost mixture. Place entire mixture in large sauce or fry pan. Cover and cook slowly until chicken is cooked through – about 15 minutes. Uncover and simmer until the sauce thickens, about 5 minutes.

Serve over rice or with tortillas
Serves: 6

Santa Fe Chicken

6 boneless skinless chicken breasts
3 TBSP lime juice
½ cup soy sauce
1 TBSP olive oil
1 TBSP chili powder
1 TBSP cumin seed
1 TBSP ground coriander
6 garlic cloves, minced
1 TBSP honey

1. Place 1 gallon freezer bag in #10 can.
2. Place chicken in bag.
3. Pour all ingredients over chicken.
4. Seal bag, shake to combine. Freeze.

To prepare: Defrost mixture. Remove chicken from marinade. Discard marinade, or put in small saucepan and heat until boiling. Grill chicken until done – baste with juices if desired. Allow to cool for 5 minutes. Slice at an angle.

Serve on tortillas topped with cheese, salsa and sour cream, if desired.

Serves: 6

Sunshine Chicken

½ cup prepared mustard
½ cup pineapple juice
2 TBSP brown sugar
6 boneless skinless chicken breasts

Ingredients needed later
12 slices lean bacon

1. Mix first 3 ingredients in a bowl until sugar is dissolved.
2. Place 1 gallon freezer bags in #10 can.
3. Place chicken in bag.
4. Pour sauce evenly over chicken.
5. Seal bag, shake to combine and freeze.

To prepare: Defrost mixture. Heat marinade in saucepan until bubbly. Wrap chicken in bacon, fastening with wooden picks. Grill chicken about 10 minutes, turning frequently and brushing with additional marinade. Remove wooden picks.

To serve, spoon remaining sauce over chicken. Serve over cooked egg noodles tossed with butter and garlic

Serves: 6

Orange Dijon Chicken

6 boneless skinless chicken breasts
1 can cream of chicken soup
¼ cup Dijon mustard
¾ cup orange juice
1 TBSP chopped fresh sage

Optional items:
6 thin slices prosciutto
6 slices mozzarella or provolone cheese
1 cup drained mandarin orange segments

1. Place 1 gallon freezer bag in #10 can.
2. Place chicken in bag.
3. Combine remaining ingredients in bowl. Stir well to combine.
4. Pour evenly over chicken.
5. Close bags, shake to combine and freeze.

To prepare: Defrost mixture. 2 options:
1. Remove chicken from marinade and grill until done. Heat marinade until bubbly. Serve over hot noodles or rice.
2. Place all items in large sauce pan or fry pan. Cover and simmer until done. Serve over hot noodles or rice.

Serves: 6

Jen's Flank Steak

1 $1/_3$ to 2 pounds flank steak
½ cup vegetable oil
¼ cup soy sauce
¼ cup red wine vinegar
2 TSP Worcestershire sauce
½ TSP ground ginger
1 TSP minced garlic

1. Place 1 gallon freezer bag in #10 can.
2. Add flank steak.
3. Pour all remaining ingredients over steak.
4. Seal bag, shake to combine and freeze.

To prepare: Defrost mixture. Remove steak from marinade; discard marinade. Preheat grill; grill steak until desired doneness is achieved.

Serve with baked potatoes and salad.

Serves: 6-8

Moroccan Marinated Steak

1 ½ pounds London broil
6 TBSP lemon juice
Handful of coriander leaves
2 garlic cloves, crushed
½ TSP cumin seeds
½ TSP paprika

1. Place 1 gallon freezer bag in #10 can.
2. Place meat in bag.
3. Pour all ingredients over steak.
4. Seal bag, shake to combine and freeze.

To prepare: Defrost mixture. Remove steak from marinade; discard marinade. Grill steak until desired doneness is achieved.

Serve with couscous and steamed butternut squash.

Serves: 6-8

Easy Goulash

1 ½ pounds ground beef
1 onion, chopped and sautéed
2 garlic cloves, minced
2 cans stewed tomatoes
1 8 oz. can mushrooms
1 TSP salt
2 TBSP Cavender's seasoning
2 TBSP Worcestershire sauce
2 TBSP red cooking wine

Ingredients needed later
2 cups water
2 cups macaroni

*If you followed the instructions given at the beginning of this chapter, the ground beef and onion will be cooked. Skip to step 2. If you did not follow those instructions, start at step 1.

1. Cook ground beef and onion until beef is no longer pink and onion is translucent; cool.
2. Place 1 gallon bag in #10 can.
3. Add all ingredients, including beef and onion, in bag.
4. Seal bag, shake to combine and freeze.

To prepare: Defrost mixture. Place contents of bag in large covered pan. Add 2 cups water and 2 cups macaroni. Cover and simmer 10-15 minutes, until pasta is done and all items are heated.

Serve with salad.

Serves: 6

BBQ Meatballs

1 pound ground beef
½ cup rolled oats
²/₃ cup milk
2 TSBP minced onion
1 TSP salt
½ TSP black pepper

Sauce:
1 ½ TBSP sugar
²/₃ cup ketchup
½ cup water
2 TBSP Worcestershire sauce
2 TBSP vinegar
4 TBSP minced onion

1. Place 1 gallon freezer bag in #10 can.
2. Combine all meatball ingredients in large bowl. Mix well.
3. Place in 1 gallon freezer bag. Seal bag and freeze.
4. Combine all sauce ingredients in sandwich size freezer bag and freeze.

To prepare: Defrost both mixtures. If desired, form mixture into balls, roll in a little flour and brown lightly in oil. Either cook meatballs on the stove top until done – topping with sauce. Or, preheat oven to 350F. Pour sauce over meatballs and bake 30-40 minutes or until done.

Serve with mashed potatoes and steamed green peas

Serves: 6-8

Spicy Tenderloin

¾ cup unsweetened pineapple juice
½ cup steak sauce
$1/3$ cup Worcestershire sauce
$1/3$ cup port wine
¼ cup lemon juice
2 TSBP seasoned salt
1 TSP black pepper
1 TSP lemon pepper
1 TSP dry mustard
2-3 pounds beef tenderloin

1. Place 1 gallon bag in #10 can.
2. Combine all ingredients, except tenderloin, in large bowl.
3. Place tenderloin in 1 gallon freezer bag.
4. Seal bag and shake to combine; freeze.

To prepare: Defrost mixture. Remove tenderloin from marinade. Cook in crock pot on high for 4-6 hours or 8-10 hours on low. To make gravy – when meat is done, remove meat from crock pot. Pour juices in to a sauce pan. In a cup, whisk to combine 3 TBSP flour and ¼ cup water. Add to sauce and heat till boiling and mixture has thickened.

Serve with green beans cooked with new red potatoes and dill.

Serves: 6-8

Smoky Barbecued Beef Brisket

1 TSP chili powder
½ TSP garlic powder
¼ TSP celery seed
$1/_8$ TSP pepper
½ cup ketchup
½ cup chili sauce

¼ cup packed brown sugar
2 TBSP vinegar
2 TBSP Worcestershire sauce
1 ½ TSP liquid smoke
½ TSP dry mustard
2-3 pounds beef brisket

Ingredients needed later
$1/_3$ cup water
3 TBSP all-purpose flour

1. In large bowl, mix all ingredients except brisket, until well combined.
2. Place 1 gallon freezer bag in #10 can
3. Place brisket in bag
4. Pour sauce over brisket. Start with 1 cup, add more until sauce is gone.
5. Seal bag, shake to combine. Freeze

To prepare: Defrost mixture. Place entire mixture in crockpot. Cool on low heat for 10-11 hours or on high heat for 5 to 5 ½ hours.
Remove meat from cooker. Place juices in a medium saucepan. In a separate bowl, stir water into flour; add to cooking juices. Cook and stir until thickened and bubbly; cook and stir for 1 minute more. Cutting across the grain, cut the brisket into thin slices.
Serve meat topped with sauce. Serve with garlic mashed potatoes and steamed peas.

Serves: 6-8

Jerk style Pork Tenderloin

½ TSP black pepper
1 TSP ground cumin
1 TSP chili powder
1 TSP cinnamon
2 TBSP olive oil
1 cup brown sugar
2 TBSP chopped garlic
1 TBSP Tabasco
2-3 pounds pork tenderloins

1. Combine first 8 ingredients in bowl.
2. Roll tenderloins in dry rub
3. Place 1 gallon freezer bag in #10 can
4. Place tenderloins in bag.
5. Seal and freeze

To prepare: Defrost mixture. Barbecue tenderloin until done. Alternately, cook in 350 oven until done.

Serve with spinach salad and citrus vinaigrette

Serves: 6-8

Zucchini Quiche

4 large eggs, beaten
1 cup milk
¼ cup sour cream
¾ cup pancake and waffle mix
3 garlic cloves, chopped
1 onion, chopped
½ green pepper, chopped
2 cups sliced zucchini
1 tomato chopped
2 TSBP Italian seasoning
1 TSP salt
¼ TSP pepper
8 oz. shredded mozzarella cheese

1. Combine eggs, milk, sour cream and pancake and waffle mix in large bowl, mix well.
2. Grease 8 x 8 pan.
3. Pour pancake and waffle mixture in pan.
4. Place all other ingredients, except cheese on top of crust.
5. Sprinkle with cheese.
6. Cover and freeze.

To prepare: Defrost mixture. Heat oven to 375F degrees. Bake for 40 minutes or until center is set. Let stand 10 minutes before serving.

Serve with fresh fruit and rolls.

Serves: 6-8

Month 4 Menu

Chicken
Thai Chicken
Chicken Balsamic
Crockpot Chicken Tarragon
Chicken Tortilla Soup
Chinese Chicken Morsels
Honey Curry Chicken

Beef
Zesty London Broil
Joes To Go
Shish Kebabs
Cilantro Lime Steak Tacos
Campfire Casserole
Asian Beef Salad

Vegetarian and Pork
Carolina Crock Pot Pork
Greek Vegetarian Crockpot Stew

Grocery List

Meat

24 chicken breasts	1 whole chicken – raw or pre-roasted
2 pounds London broil or flank steak	2 pounds ground beef
2 pounds top sirloin steak	2 pounds flank steak
1 ½ pounds top round steak	2 pounds. chicken thighs, skin removed
2 pounds pork shoulder roast	

Canned items

1 8 oz. cans mushrooms and stems	14 ½ oz. can diced tomatoes
4 oz. can chopped green chilies	4 oz. can chopped jalapenos
1 cup + 2 TBSP lemon juice	¼ cup lime juice
8 oz. tomato sauce	¾ cup salsa
½ cup green chili salsa	14 ½ oz. can Mexican style tomatoes
2 16 oz. cans pinto beans	$1/_3$ cup sliced black olives
2 6 oz. cans tomato paste	14 oz. can coconut milk
2 15 oz. cans Navy beans	

Refrigerated items

¼ cup butter	½ cup apple juice
1 lemon	

Fresh fruit and vegetables

3 bulbs garlic	5 onions
1 bunch cilantro	6 oz. snow peas
8 oz. baby carrots	fresh ginger

Seasonings

¼ cup dry sherry	taco seasoning
Sweet hot oriental chili sauce	$1/_3$ cup chili sauce
$1/_3$ cup Worcestershire sauce	Sesame seed oil

Kitchen Staples

vegetable oil	$1/3$ cup balsamic vinegar (white if possible)
chicken bouillon	sugar
Italian seasoning	garlic salt
chili powder	cumin
$3/4$ cup soy sauce	$3/4$ cup Dijon mustard
$1/3$ cup honey	curry powder
cayenne pepper	ginger
pepper	salt
$1/3$ cup brown sugar	white vinegar
red wine vinegar	corn starch
flour	cider vinegar
coriander	peanut butter
dry tarragon	dry parsley
prepared yellow mustard	cinnamon
dry mustard	

NB – all fresh ingredients that are needed later are not listed on the grocery list. You will want to buy these fresh as you need them.

Storage Containers Needed

14 1 gallon freezer bags

You will also need 1 or more #10 cans. You will use this can for holding your storage bag as you place the food in the bag.

#10 cans are found in the industrial size food areas in grocery stores. You can also find these cans in warehouse stores. They typically hold 6 or 7 pounds of canned food. Buy one can of something you can use, after removing and using the food, wash the can and keep on hand for each month's cooking.

I normally have 2 or 3 of these cans on hand, so I can prepare more than 1 recipe at a time.

Preparations needed before assembling dishes

- Brown ground beef for Joes to Go and Campfire Casserole
- Sauté onions for Thai Chicken, Chicken Tortilla Soup, Joes to Go, Cilantro Lime Steak, Campfire Casserole, Carolina Crock Pot Pork and Greek Vegetarian Crockpot Stew.
- Cook whole chicken for Chicken Tortilla Soup. Cool and cut up. Alternately, you can use pre-roasted chicken which you debone and cut up into bite size pieces.
- Cube meat for Shish Kebabs and Asian Beef Salad
- Melt butter for Honey Curry Chicken
- Before assembling meals, label all bags with the name of the recipe. Use a permanent marker.
- Assemble meals in whichever order you choose.
- Promptly freeze meals to avoid any potential illness.

Thai Chicken

2 TBSP vegetable oil
1 medium onion, chopped
1 garlic clove, minced
1 TSP coriander
1 TSP cumin
1 TSP salt
2 TSP grated fresh ginger
2-3 TSP sweet hot oriental chili sauce
2 TBSP soy sauce
2 TBSP peanut butter
14 oz. can coconut milk
2 pounds chicken thighs, skin removed

If you followed the directions at the beginning of the chapter, the onion will be sautéed, please add onion and remaining seasonings in to pan and continue on with directions. If you did not pre-sauté onions, do so now.

1. Sauté onion, garlic, coriander, cumin, salt and ginger in oil.
2. Add hot oriental chili sauce, soy sauce, peanut butter and coconut milk. Stir and heat until bubbly. Cool completely.
3. Place 1 gallon freezer bag in #10 can
4. Add chicken and pour sauce over top.
5. Seal bag and shake to combine. Freeze

To prepare: Defrost mixture completely. Place entire mixture in crock pot and cook on low 5-6 hours or on high 2-3 hours. Alternately, place chicken and sauce in large oven proof pan and cook for 1 hour at 325F.

Serve with steamed rice.

Serves: 6

Chicken Balsamic

6 boneless skinless chicken breasts
4 TSP vegetable oil
$1/_3$ cup balsamic vinegar (use white balsamic if possible)
½ cup chicken bouillon (1 TSP bouillon, ½ cup water)
2 TBSP sugar
1 garlic clove crushed (½ TSP)
1 TSP dried Italian seasoning

1. Place 1 gallon freezer bag in #10 can.
2. Place chicken in bag.
3. Pour remaining ingredients over chicken. Seal bag, shake to combine.

To prepare: Defrost mixture. Remove chicken from marinade. Either discard the marinade or place in small sauce pan and boil. Cook chicken in large skillet over medium high heat until chicken is cooked through. Alternately, cook on barbecue grill and baste with marinade in the last 10 minutes of cooking.

Serve with spinach salad and saffron rice.

Serves: 6

Crockpot Chicken Tarragon

6 boneless skinless chicken breasts
2 TBSP butter
1 TSP garlic salt
1 TSP tarragon
1 TBSP dried parsley
$1/_8$ TSP black pepper

Ingredients needed later
2 tablespoons corn starch
1 cup accumulated cooking liquid (if necessary add chicken
broth to make one cup)

1. Place 1 gallon freezer bag in #10 can
2. Pour all ingredients in bag. Seal and shake to combine. Freeze.

To prepare: Defrost mixture. Add entire mixture to 6 qt. crockpot. Cook on low 8 hours or 4 hours on high. When done, remove chicken and place on platter. If desired, make gravy by combining 2 TBSP cornstarch in 2 TBSP cold water. Stir until smooth. In a saucepan, combine cornstarch mixture with 1 cup of chicken liquid. Heat and stir until mixture boils and thickens.

Serve with white rice and gravy made from chicken juices.

Serves: 6

Chicken Tortilla Soup

½ cup onion, chopped and sautéed
3 cups, cooked chicken (see note)
1 TSP vegetable oil
1 garlic clove, pressed
½ TSP chili powder
½ TSP ground cumin
2 TBSP chicken broth powder
1 can (14 ½ oz.) diced tomatoes, undrained
1 can (4 oz.) chopped green chilies, undrained
1 can (4 oz.) chopped jalapenos, undrained - optional

*If you followed the instructions at the beginning of this chapter, onion will already be sautéed and the chicken will be cooked, cooled and cut up, then start with step 3. If not, please start at the beginning of this recipe.

1. Sauté onion and cool
2. Boil or cook chicken; cool and cut up
3. Place 1 gallon freezer bag in #10 can.
4. Pour all ingredients in bag. Seal and shake to combine. Freeze.

To prepare: Defrost mixture. Pour entire contents of bag in to medium sauce pan; add 4 cups water. Heat until bubbly.

Serve topped with tortillas and sour cream, if desired.

Note: 1 boiled or pre-roasted chicken will give you 3 cups chopped chicken. This recipe can use up to 3 cups of chicken, if desired.

Serves: 6

Chinese Chicken Morsels

6 boneless skinless chicken breasts
1 cup lemon juice
½ cup soy sauce
½ cup Dijon mustard
1 TBSP vegetable oil
½ TSP cayenne pepper

1. Place 1 gallon bag in #10 can.
2. Place chicken breasts in bag.
3. Pour marinade ingredients over chicken. Seal and shake to mix; freeze.

To prepare: Defrost mixture. Remove chicken from marinade. Heat marinade in sauce pan until bubbly. Grill chicken on grill until done, basting occasionally with sauce.

Serve with rice and extra sauce. Alternately, cut up chicken and serve on a bed over greens and add chow mein noodles.

Serves: 6

Honey Curry Chicken

$1/3$ cup melted butter or margarine
6 boneless skinless chicken breasts
$1/3$ cup honey
¼ cup Dijon mustard
2 TSBP curry powder
Pinch cayenne

*If you followed the instructions at the beginning of this chapter, the butter will be melted and cooled, then start with step 2. If not, please start at the beginning of this recipe.

1. Melt butter, set aside to cool.
2. Place 1 gallon freezer bag in #10 can.
3. Place chicken in bag.
4. Mix remaining ingredients in bowl.
5. Pour all other ingredients over chicken. Seal bag, shake to combine; freeze.

To prepare: Defrost mixture. Place chicken and marinade in large covered stir-fry pan. Cook covered until chicken is done. Alternately, grill on barbecue until chicken is done. Baste occasionally with sauce.

Serve with steamed mixed vegetables and with rice.

Serves: 6

Zesty London Broil

1 TSP ground ginger
1 TBSP grated lemon zest
1 TBSP vegetable oil
1 garlic clove minced
1 TSP black pepper
1 TSP brown sugar
2 pounds London broil or Flank Steak

1. Place 1 gallon freezer bag in #10 can
2. In a small bowl, combine all ingredients except steak.
3. Rub marinade ingredients into steak.
4. Put steak in bag and freeze

To prepare: Defrost steak. Grill until desired doneness is achieved.

Serve with baked potato and steamed broccoli.

Serves: 6

Joes To Go

1 pound lean ground beef, browned (2 cups)
½ cup finely chopped onion, sautéed
1 ½ TSP garlic salt
½ TSP pepper
½ cup chili sauce
¼ cup brown sugar
1 TBSP white vinegar
1 TBSP prepared mustard
1 8 oz. can tomato sauce

*If you followed the instructions at the beginning of this chapter, the ground beef and onion will already be sautéed, then start with step 2. If not, please start at the beginning of this recipe.

1. Brown ground beef and onion. Drain, cool completely before continuing.
2. Place 1 gallon freezer bag in #10 can
3. Combine all ingredients in medium bowl.
4. Place ingredients in bag. Seal bag and freeze.

To prepare: Defrost mixture, simmer uncovered for 10 minutes, stirring occasionally.

Serve on hamburger buns. Serve with potato salad, carrot and celery sticks.

Serves: 6

Shish Kebabs

2 pounds cubed, boneless top sirloin steak
¾ cup coarsely chopped salsa
1 4 oz. can green chili salsa
1 ½ TSP chili powder
1 TBSP vegetable oil
¼ cup red wine vinegar
¼ TSP salt

Ingredients needed later
White Onion
Green bell pepper
Pineapple
Tomatoes
Mushrooms

*If you followed the instructions at the beginning of this chapter, the meat will already be cubed, then start with step 2. If not, please start at the beginning of this recipe.

1. Cube steak into bite size pieces
2. Place 1 gallon freezer bag in #10 can.
3. Place all ingredients in bag.
4. Shake to combine and freeze.

To prepare: Defrost mixture. Remove meat from marinade. Cut desired vegetables into thick pieces to put on a skewer. Alternate meat, vegetable and pineapple on the skewer. Barbecue until done.

Serve with rice.

Serves: 6

Cilantro Lime Steak Tacos

2 TBSP chopped onion - sautéed
Juice of 3 limes (about ¼ cup)
2 TSP salt
1 TSP pepper
1 ½ cups chopped cilantro
2 TBSP vegetable oil
2 pounds flank steak

*If you followed the instructions at the beginning of this chapter, the onion will already be sautéed, then start with step 2. If not, please start at the beginning of this recipe.

1. Sauté onion and cool completely.
2. Place 1 gallon freezer bag in #10 can.
3. Place all ingredients, except steak, in food processor. Process until smooth.
4. Place flank steak in bag
5. Pour marinade over steak and freeze.

To prepare: Defrost mixture. Remove steak from marinade; discard marinade. Grill until desired doneness is achieved.

When done, cut steak on diagonal into slices about $1/8$ to ¼ inch thick.
Serve in taco shells with lettuce, tomato, steak strips, cheese and salsa. Squeeze juice of half a lime over each taco. Alternately, serve on salad.

Serves: 6

Campfire Casserole

1 pound ground beef, browned (2 cups)
½ cup onion, chopped and sautéed
3 TBSP dry taco seasoning
1 TBSP water
1 14.5 oz. can Mexican-style tomatoes – chopped
2 16 oz. cans pinto beans
$^1/_3$ cup ripe olives, sliced

Ingredients needed later
4 oz. Monterey Jack cheese – shredded
1 package cornbread mix – prepared

*If you followed the instructions at the beginning of this chapter, the ground beef and onion will already be sautéed, then start with step 2. If not, please start at the beginning of this recipe.

1. Sauté ground beef and onion. Cool completely before proceeding with step 2.
2. Place 1 gallon freezer bag in #10 can.
3. Combine beef, onion, seasoning, water, tomatoes, pinto beans and olives in bag, shake well and freeze.

To prepare: Defrost mixture. Preheat oven to 350 degrees. Place in 3 qt. casserole dish. Sprinkle with cheese and top with prepared cornbread mix. Bake for 15 minutes or until lightly browned.

Serves: 6

Asian Beef Salad

1 ½ pounds top round steak, cut into strips
8 oz. canned mushrooms
6 oz. snow peas
¼ cup dry sherry
¼ cup soy sauce
1 TBSP freshly grated ginger
2 (or more) garlic cloves pressed
1 TBSP sesame seed oil
2 TBSP cornstarch

Ingredients needed later
6 cups spinach leaves
Chow mein noodles
Water chestnuts

*If you followed the instructions at the beginning of this chapter, the steak will already be cut into strips, then start with step 2. If not, please start at the beginning of this recipe.

1. Cut steak into strips.
2. Place 1 gallon freezer bag in #10 can
3. Place meat strips, mushrooms and snow peas in bag.
4. Combine sherry, soy sauce, ginger, garlic, sesame seed oil and cornstarch in a mixing bowl. Stir to combine.
5. Pour marinade over meat mixture. Seal bag, shake to combine and freeze.

To prepare: Defrost mixture. Place mixture in large stir-fry pan. Cook until meat is done and sauce is cooked and thickened. Let cool slightly.

To serve: Place spinach on each plate, serve beef mixture on top. Garnish with chow mein noodles, water chestnuts and other items, as desired.

Serves: 6

Carolina Crock Pot Pork

¾ cup onion – chopped and sautéed
1 TBSP olive oil
2 pounds pork shoulder roast
2 cloves garlic, chopped
1 ½ TSP dry mustard
$1/_3$ cup tomato paste
¼ cup Worcestershire sauce
3 TBSP cider vinegar

*If you followed the instructions at the beginning of this chapter, the onion will already be sautéed, then start with step 2. If not, please start at the beginning of this recipe.

1. Using the olive oil, sauté the onion. Cool completely before continuing.
2. Place 1 gallon bag in #10 can.
3. Place all items in bag. Seal bag, shake and freeze.

To prepare: Place all items in crock pot. Cook on high for 5-7 hours. Cool, then shred with 2 forks and serve with juice. Serve on buns, if desired.

Serve on buns with coleslaw or potato salad.

Serves: 6-8

Greek Vegetarian Crockpot Stew

1 TBSP vegetable oil
2 medium onions, cut into 6 thin wedges and sautéed
2 15 oz. cans Navy Beans
2 TBSP flour
8 oz. baby carrots
1 6 oz. can tomato paste
½ cup apple juice
3 TBSP water
2 TBSP lemon juice
1 TSP cumin
½ TSP cinnamon
1 TSP honey

Optional ingredient
$^1/_3$ cup crumbled Feta cheese

*If you followed the instructions at the beginning of this chapter, the onion will already be sautéed, then start with step 2. If not, please start at the beginning of this recipe.

1. Using the vegetable oil, sauté the onions. Cool completely before continuing.
2. Drain and rinse beans.
3. Place 1 gallon freezer bag in #10 can.
4. Combine all ingredients in bag. Seal bag, shake to combine and freeze.

To prepare: Defrost mixture. Place in crockpot and cook on low 6-7 hours or until well cooked. Sprinkle with cheese if desired.

Serve with brown rice and spinach salad.

Serves: 6-8

Month 5 Menu

Chicken
White Lightning Chicken Chili
Sweet and Sour Chicken
Pizza Chicken Italiano
Mandarin Orange Chicken
Indonesian Chicken Satay
Honey Lime Grilled Chicken

Beef
Ground Beef Stroganoff
Smoky Barbecued Beef Brisket
Balsamic Flank Steak
Adobo Steak
BBQ Mini Meatloaves
Jerk Beef Tenderloin

Vegetarian and Pork
Sausage Rice Skillet
Chili Rellenos Casserole

Grocery List

Meat

2 whole chickens - raw or pre-roasted	24 chicken breasts
2 pounds ground beef	3 pounds beef tenderloin
2 pounds flank steak	2 pounds beef sirloin steaks
1 pound Polska kielbasa	2-3 pounds beef brisket

Canned items

3 cans (15 oz. ea.) Great northern beans	1 TBSP lemon juice
lime juice $^2/_3$ cup	13 ½ oz. can pineapple chunks
2 16 oz. cans tomato sauce	6 oz. frozen orange juice
3 8 oz. can sliced mushrooms	½ cup teriyaki sauce
16 oz. can diced stewed tomatoes	¾ cup balsamic vinaigrette salad dressing
chipotle peppers in adobo sauce	1 cup quick cooking oats
¾ cup barbecue sauce	2 TBSP Italian salad dressing
3 cups brown rice (dry)	7 oz. can whole green chilies

Refrigerated items and Fresh fruit and veggies

3 bulbs garlic	6 whole onions
2 fresh jalapenos	5 large carrots
3 eggs	1 stalk celery
1 cup half and half	½ lb. Monterey Jack cheese, grated
½ lb. sharp cheddar cheese,	2 TBSP butter

Seasonings and Kitchen Staples

vegetable oil	cumin
½ cup sugar	½ cup cider vinegar
2 TBSP corn starch	2 ⅓ TBSP soy sauce
oregano	garlic salt
onion powder	½ cup flour
½ cup honey	salt
pepper	¾ cup ketchup
chicken bouillon	beef bouillon
½ TSP Tabasco sauce	⅓ cup brown sugar
coriander	ginger
chili powder	garlic powder
2 TBSP white vinegar	2 TBSP Worcestershire sauce
1 ½ TSP liquid smoke	½ cup olive oil
celery seed	½ cup chili sauce
4 TBSP Jamaican jerk seasoning	4 Bay leaves
dry mustard	red pepper flakes

NB – all fresh ingredients that are needed later are not listed on the grocery list. You will want to buy these fresh as you need them.

Storage Containers Needed

13 1 gallon freezer bags
1 8 x 8 freezer to oven pan – can be plastic or aluminum. Must have a lid.

You will also need 1 or more #10 cans. You will use this can for holding your storage bag as you place the food in the bag.
#10 cans are found in the industrial size food areas in grocery stores. You can also find these cans in warehouse stores. They typically hold 6 or 7 pounds of canned food. Buy one can of something you can use, after removing and using the food, wash the can and keep on hand for each month's cooking.
I normally have 2 or 3 of these cans on hand, so I can prepare more than 1 recipe at a time.

Preparations needed before assembling dishes

- Boil whole chickens for White lightning chicken chili and Sweet and Sour Chicken. After chicken is boiled, cool and debone. Cut up in to bite size pieces. Alternately, use pre-roasted chickens and debone and chop in to bite size pieces.
- Chop all onions and sauté until translucent. Use ¼ cup butter per onion.
- Sauté jalapenos for White Lightning chicken chili – use 1 TSP vegetable oil
- Brown ground beef for Ground Beef Stroganoff. Drain and cool
- Follow directions to create sauce for Sweet and Sour chicken. Cool completely before bagging.
- Follow directions for Mandarin Orange Chicken sauce. Cool sauce completely before bagging.
- Before assembling meals, label all bags with the name of the recipe. Use a permanent marker.
- Assemble meals in whichever order you choose.
- Promptly freeze meals to avoid any potential illness.

White Lightning Chicken Chili

3 cups cooked chicken – boiled or pre-roasted
6 garlic cloves
1 cup onion, chopped
¼ cup fresh jalapeno peppers, seeded and chopped
3 - 15 oz. cans Great Northern beans, drained, rinsed and
  divided
2 TSP vegetable oil
2 TBSP chicken bouillon
1 ½ TSP ground cumin
¼ cup lime juice

Ingredients needed later
6 cups water
1 TBSP cornstarch
1 TBSP cold water

*If you followed the instructions at the beginning of this chapter, the chicken, onion and jalapeno will already be sautéed, then start with step 3. If not, please start at the beginning of this recipe.

1. Boil chicken. Cool completely and cut up.
2. Chop onion and jalapeno peppers. Heat oil in large sauce pan, over medium heat; sauté 4-5 minutes or until onion is tender, then cool.
3. Drain both cans of beans, place 1in a bowl, add garlic and mash together using a potato masher. Place 1 gallon freezer bag in #10 can
4. Place all ingredients in 1 gallon freezer bag. Seal bag and shake to combine. Freeze.

To prepare: Defrost mixture. Place contents of entire bag in large sauce pan, add 6 cups water and heat for 20-25 minutes. Combine cornstarch and water, stirring until smooth. Add cornstarch mixture to chili; cook 5 minutes, stirring constantly, until slightly thickened.

Serves: 8

Sweet and Sour Chicken

2 cups cubed, cooked chicken
2 TBSP vegetable oil
1 13 ½ oz. can pineapple chunks, drained (reserve juice)
½ cup sugar
½ cup cider vinegar
2 TBSP corn starch
$1/3$ cup water
1 TSP soy sauce
4 large carrots, cooked and cut in 1 inch pieces

*If you followed the instructions at the beginning of this chapter, the chicken will already be cooked and sauce will be made, then start with step 5. If not, please start at the beginning of this recipe.

1. Brown chicken pieces in oil; remove and set aside. Cool completely
2. Drain pineapple, reserve juice. Add enough water to reserved pineapple juice to make 1 cup.
3. Add pineapple juice and water to skillet along with sugar and vinegar. Heat to boiling, stirring constantly. Reduce heat; cover and simmer 2 minutes.
4. Blend 2 TBSP corn starch and water; stir into skillet. Heat, stirring constantly, until mixture thickens and boils; cook 1 minute.
5. To sauce, add in pineapple chunks, soy sauce, carrots and chicken pieces. Cool completely.
6. Place 1 gallon freezer bag in #10 can
7. Place all ingredients in 1 gallon freezer bag. Seal bag and shake to combine. Freeze.

To prepare: Defrost mixture. Heat in large sauce pan until bubbly.

Serve with steamed white rice and stir fry vegetables.

Serves: 6

Pizza Chicken Italiano

1 15 oz. can tomato sauce
1 ½ TSP oregano
½ TSP garlic salt
½ TSP onion powder
½ TSP sugar
6 boneless skinless chicken breasts

Ingredients Needed Later
1 2 ½ oz. can sliced ripe olives, drained
4 oz. shredded Mozzarella cheese

1. In medium bowl, combine tomato sauce and all spices.
2. Place 1 gallon freezer bag in #10 can
3. Place chicken breasts in bag and pour sauce over top. Seal bag and shake to combine; freeze.

To prepare: Defrost mixture. Preheat oven to 425F. Place mixture in 9 x 9 oven proof pan and cover with foil. Bake for 15-20 minutes – check for doneness. Remove foil, top with olives and cheese and continue to bake, uncovered for an additional 10 minutes.

Serve with a side salad and pasta tossed with butter and garlic

Serves: 6

Mandarin Orange Chicken

2 TSP all-purpose flour
$^2/_3$ cup water
6 oz. frozen orange juice concentrate (not reconstituted)
2 TSP chicken bouillon
6 boneless skinless chicken breasts
1 8 oz. can sliced mushrooms

Ingredients Needed Later
11 oz. can mandarin orange sections

*If you followed the instructions at the beginning of this chapter, the sauce will be made, then start with step 2. If not, please start at the beginning of this recipe.

1. Combine flour, water, orange juice and bouillon in large sauce pan. Cook until slightly thickened. Cool completely.
2. Place 1 gallon freezer bag in #10 can
3. Add chicken and cooled orange juice mixture. Seal bag, shake to combine; freeze

To prepare: Defrost mixture. Cook chicken in marinade in large fry pan until cooked through and bubbly.

Serve over rice. Add drained mandarin oranges, if desired.

Serves: 6

Honey Lime Grilled Chicken

6 boneless skinless chicken breasts
½ cup honey
3 TBSP lime juice
2 TBSP soy sauce
2 garlic cloves minced

1. Place 1 gallon freezer bag in #10 can
2. Place chicken breasts in bag.
3. Combine all remaining ingredients in small bowl; pour over chicken. Seal bag and shake to combine, freeze.

To prepare: Defrost mixture. Remove chicken from marinade. Heat marinade until bubbling. Grill chicken, basting frequently with marinade.

Serve with salad, saffron rice

Serves: 6

Indonesian Chicken Satay

2 TBSP butter,
1 TBSP lemon juice
½ TSP Tabasco
3 TBSP grated onion
1 TBSP brown sugar
1 TSP coriander
½ TSP ground cumin
¼ TSP ginger
1 garlic clove, crushed
½ cup teriyaki sauce or soy sauce
6 boneless skinless chicken breasts

*If you followed the instructions at the beginning of this chapter, the sauce will be made, then start with step 2. If not, please start at the beginning of this recipe.

1. In large sauce pan, melt butter and add remaining ingredients, except chicken. Bring to a boil and simmer 5 minutes. Cool completely.
2. Place 1 gallon freezer bag in #10 can.
3. Place chicken breasts in bag and pour sauce over top. Seal bag and shake to combine; freeze.

To prepare: defrost completely. There are 2 choices for preparation:
1. Remove chicken from sauce and barbecue. Boil sauce and then brush chicken with sauce.
2. Remove chicken from sauce, cut up in to 1 inch cubes. Thread on to wooden skewers. Boil sauce marinade BBQ chicken until done, brushing occasionally with marinade.

Serve with steamed rice and stir fry vegetables

Serves: 6

Ground Beef Stroganoff

1 pound lean ground beef
½ TSP salt
¼ TSP freshly ground black pepper
¼ cup chopped yellow onions
8 oz. can sliced mushrooms
1 garlic minced
2 TSP beef bouillon
¼ cup ketchup

Ingredients Needed Later
2 cups water
½ cup sour cream
½ pound small elbow macaroni or wide egg noodles, cooked

 *If you followed the instructions at the beginning of this chapter, the ground beef and onion will already be sautéed, then start at step 2. If you did not use the previous instructions, start with step 1.

1. Heat large skillet to medium. Add ground beef and onion. Season with salt and pepper. Cook until onion is translucent and beef is no longer pink. Drain and cool.
2. Place 1 gallon freezer bag in #10 can
3. Place all ingredients in 1 gallon freezer bag. Seal bag and shake to combine. Freeze.

To prepare: Defrost mixture. Place in large skillet; add 2 cups water and sour cream. Heat until boiling and slightly thickened. Either mix in pasta or serve over pasta.

Serves: 6

Smoky Barbecued Beef Brisket

1 TSP chili powder
½ TSP garlic powder
¼ TSP celery seed
$^1/_8$ TSP pepper
½ cup ketchup
½ cup chili sauce
¼ cup packed brown sugar
2 TBSP vinegar
2 TBSP Worcestershire sauce
1 ½ TSP liquid smoke
½ TSP dry mustard
2-3 pounds beef brisket

Ingredients needed later
$^1/_3$ cup water
3 TBSP all-purpose flour

1. In large bowl, mix all ingredients except brisket, until well combined.
2. Place 1 gallon freezer bag in #10 can
3. Place all ingredients in 1 gallon freezer bag. Seal bag and shake to combine. Freeze.

To prepare: Defrost mixture. Place entire mixture in crockpot. Cool on low heat for 10-11 hours or on high heat for 5 to 5 ½ hours.
Remove meat from cooker. Skim and discard fat from juice in cooker; measure 2 ½ cups juices. In a medium saucepan stir water into flour; add cooking juices. Cook and stir until thickened and bubbly; cook and stir for 1 minute more. Cutting across the grain, cut the brisket into thin slices.
Serve meat topped with sauce. Serve with garlic mashed potatoes and steamed peas.

Serves: 6

Balsamic Marinated Flank Steak

¾ cup balsamic vinaigrette salad dressing
4 garlic cloves pressed
1 ½ TSP dried oregano leaves
Dash ground black pepper
½ TSP dried red pepper flakes
1 ½- 2 pounds flank steak

1. Combine dressing, garlic, oregano and peppers in bowl.
2. Place 1 gallon freezer bag in #10 can
3. Place steak in 1 gallon freezer bag, add dressing. Seal bag, shake to combine; freeze.

To prepare: defrost steak, remove from bag and discard marinade. If desired, reserve marinade and heat until boiling, then brush steak as cooking. Preheat barbecue and cook steak over medium heat 5-10 minutes on one side and turn over and cook until desired doneness on the other side.

Serve with baked potatoes and green salad

Serves: 6

Adobo Steak

¼ cup lime juice
3 garlic cloves minced
1 TSP oregano
1 TSP ground cumin
2 TBSP finely chopped chipotle peppers in adobo sauce
4 8 oz. beef sirloin steaks

1. Mix the lime juice, garlic, oregano, and cumin in a small bowl. Stir in chipotle peppers, and season to taste with adobo sauce.
2. Place 1 gallon freezer bag in #10 can
3. With a sharp knife pierce the meat on both sides, sprinkle with salt and pepper
4. Place all ingredients in 1 gallon freezer bag. Seal bag and shake to combine. Freeze.

To prepare: Defrost mixture. Discard marinade. Heat grill to medium. Place steak on grill, cook until desired doneness is achieved.

Serve with mashed potatoes mixed with adobo sauce.

Serves: 6-8

Jerk Beef Tenderloin

½ cup olive oil
4 TBSP dried Jamaican jerk seasoning
2 TBSP balsamic vinegar
4 small bay leaves, crumbled finely
3 minced garlic cloves
3 pounds beef tenderloin

1. Place 1 gallon freezer bag in #10 can
2. Place all ingredients in 1 gallon freezer bag. Seal bag and shake to combine. Freeze

To prepare: Defrost mixture. Preheat oven to 400. Remove tenderloin from marinade. Discard marinade, if desired; alternately heat until boiling and use as a gravy. Place tenderloin on large rimmed baking sheet and sprinkle with salt and pepper. Cook for 1 hour. Remove from oven and allow to rest for 5 minutes before slicing.
Serve with basmati rice and gravy, if desired

Serves: 6-8

BBQ Mini Meatloaves

1 pound ground beef
1 cup quick cooking oats
¾ cup barbecue sauce
1 egg
2 TBSP Italian salad dressing
1 ½ TSP salt
1 ½ TSP pepper

1. Combine all ingredients in a medium size bowl
2. Place 1 gallon freezer bag in #10 can
3. Add mixture to bag. Seal bag and freeze.

To prepare: Defrost mixture. Form in to patties and barbecue on grill or cook on the stove top in a skillet. Alternately, heat oven to 350, place mixture in pie pan and cook for 20-25 minutes or until cooked through. Top with additional barbecue sauce in the last 5 minutes of cooking.

Serve with mashed potatoes and salad. Or serve on hamburger buns.

Serves: 6

Sausage Rice Skillet

6 cups cooked brown rice (use 3 cups dry to cook up to 6 cups)
1 large onion, chopped and sautéed
½ cup carrots, sliced
1 garlic clove pressed
1 large stalk celery, chopped
8 oz. canned mushrooms
1 14½ oz. can diced tomatoes (with juice)
Salt to taste
¼ TSP dry mustard
1 TSP cumin
1 lb. Polska kielbasa, sliced

 *If you followed the instructions at the beginning of this chapter, the onion will already be sautéed, then start at step 2. If you did not use the previous instructions, start with step 1.

1. Sautee onion in 1 TSP oil.
2. Place rice in 1 gallon freezer bag, seal.
3. Place 1 gallon freezer bag in #10 can.
4. Combine all remaining ingredients and place in 2nd freezer bag. Seal and shake to combine. Freeze both bags together.

To prepare: Defrost mixture. Simmer sausage mixture 15-20 minutes. Add rice to skillet and stir to heat through and simmer another 5 minutes.
Serve with salad.

Serves: 6

Chile Rellenos Casserole

1 cup half and half
2 eggs
$^1/_3$ cup flour
7 oz. can whole green chilies
½ pound Monterey Jack cheese, grated
½ pound sharp cheddar cheese, grated
8 oz. can tomato sauce

1. Lightly butter or grease an 8 x 8 freezer safe container
2. Beat half and half with the eggs and flour until smooth.
3. Split open the chilies rinse out the seeds and drain on paper towels.
4. Mix cheeses together. Reserve ½ cup for topping.
5. Alternate layers of egg mixture, chilies and cheese
6. Pour the tomato sauce over the top and sprinkle with the remaining cheese.
7. Cover and freeze

To prepare: Defrost mixture. Preheat oven to 350. Remove lid from pan. Bake for 1 hour or until done in the center.

Serve with warm tortillas and green salad.

Serves: 6

Month 6 Menu

Chicken
Grilled Mojo Chicken
Curry Chicken and Broccoli
Grilled Seasoned Chicken
Margarita Chicken
Mexican Chicken Lasagna
Chicken and Artichoke Casserole

Beef
Port marinated Top Sirloin
Brisket with Cranberry Gravy
5 Bean Bake
Stuffed Peppers
Montreal Flank Steak
Sesame Beef Tenderloin

Vegetarian and Pork
Easy Black Bean Chili
Apricot Glazed Pork Medallions

Grocery List

Meat

3 whole chickens – raw or pre-roasted	18 chicken breasts
3 pounds top sirloin	3 pounds beef brisket
3 pounds ground beef	2-3 pounds beef tenderloin
2-3 pounds flank steak	2 pounds pork tenderloin

Canned items

½ cup orange juice concentrate	10 oz. can condensed cream of chicken soup
$1/_3$ cup lime juice	½ cup mayonnaise
2 8 oz. can mushroom pieces	½ cup prepared Italian salad dressing
$1/_3$ cup lemon juice	
5 16 oz. (80 oz.) can diced stewed tomatoes	½ cup salsa
4 cans black beans	10 lasagna noodles
1 8 oz. can chopped green chilies	1 can (2 cups) artichokes hearts, in water
1 $1/_3$ cups port wine	1 can (2 cups) whole berry cranberry sauce
7 cups (56 oz.) tomato sauce	2 TBSP Dijon mustard
1 can (2 cups) Great Northern beans	2 cans (4 cups) pork and beans
2 cups honey Dijon barbecue sauce	2 cups rice (will yield 4 cups cooked)
1 12 oz. can limeade	$2/_3$ cup tequila
2 15oz cans cut green beans	Hot pepper sauce (like Tabasco)
2 ½ cups (20 oz.) apricot preserves	2 TBSP fresh or pickled ginger

Refrigerated items and Fresh fruit and veggies

5 bulbs garlic	Fresh mint
1 ¾ cups grated Parmesan cheese	2 cup chopped frozen broccoli
4 onions	16 oz. ricotta cheese
1 egg	6 oz. Monterey Jack cheese, grated
½ cup butter	1 ½ cups cream
2 shallots	1 bunch cilantro
Green bell pepper	2 carrots
½ cup butter	1 jalapeno

Seasonings and Kitchen Staples

vegetable oil	1 cup olive oil
curry powder	chili powder
garlic powder	1 ¼ cups soy sauce
oregano	ground ginger
1 pkg. taco seasoning	½ cup flour
honey	salt
pepper	rosemary
chicken bouillon	2 TBSP brown sugar
2 TBSP red wine vinegar	1 TBSP Montreal steak seasoning
¼ cup balsamic vinegar	

NB – all fresh ingredients that are needed later are not listed on the grocery list. You will want to buy these fresh as you need them.

Storage Containers Needed

13 1 gallon freezer bags
1 9 x 13 freezer to oven pan – can be plastic or aluminum. Must have a lid.

You will also need 1 or more #10 cans. You will use this can for holding your storage bag as you place the food in the bag.
#10 cans are found in the industrial size food areas in grocery stores. You can also find these cans in warehouse stores. They typically hold 6 or 7 pounds of canned food. Buy one can of something you can use, after removing and using the food, wash the can and keep on hand for each month's cooking.
I normally have 2 or 3 of these cans on hand, so I can prepare more than 1 recipe at a time.

Preparations needed before assembling dishes

- Boil whole chickens for Curry Chicken Broccoli, Chicken and artichoke casserole and Mexican Chicken Lasagna. After chicken is boiled, cool and debone. Cut up in to bite size pieces. Alternately use a pre-roasted chicken and debone and chop in to bite size pieces.
- Chop all onions and sauté until translucent. Use ¼ cup butter per onion, or 1-2 TBSP vegetable oil.
- Chop green bell pepper and sauté until translucent. Use 1-2 TBSP vegetable oil.
- Brown ground beef for 5 Bean Bake and Stuffed Peppers. Drain and cool
- Follow directions to create sauce for Chicken Artichoke Casserole. Cool completely before bagging.
- Cook rice for Stuffed Peppers; cool
- Before assembling meals, label all bags with the name of the recipe. Use a permanent marker.
- Assemble meals in whichever order you choose.
- Promptly freeze meals to avoid any potential illness.

Grilled Mojo Chicken

6 boneless skinless chicken breasts
½ cup orange juice concentrate (not reconstituted)
$^1/_3$ cup lime juice
2 garlic cloves, minced
1 TBSP fresh mint, chopped
1 TSP dried oregano
1 TSP ground ginger
½ TSP salt
½ TSP pepper
2 TBSP olive oil

Ingredients needed later
¼ cup olive oil
3 oranges
1 bunch asparagus
12 cups mixed salad greens

1. Place 1 gallon freezer bag in #10 can.
2. Add all ingredients to bag.
3. Seal, shake to combine; freeze.

To prepare: Defrost mixture. Remove chicken from marinade. Heat marinade until boiling. Grill chicken until done.

To finish – Steam or grill asparagus. Cool marinade. Whisk ¾ cup marinade with ¼ cup olive oil to create salad dressing. Peel and section oranges. Cut chicken crosswise into ½ inch slices. Toss greens, oranges, salt and pepper with most of the dressing. Arrange salad in six shallow bowls. Place chicken and asparagus over each. Drizzle with remaining dressing.

Serves: 6

Curry Chicken Broccoli

10 oz. can condensed cream of chicken soup
½ cup mayonnaise
¾ TSP curry powder
¾ cup grated Parmesan cheese
2 cups chopped frozen broccoli
3 cups cooked, chopped chicken
8 oz. can mushroom pieces

1. Mix 1st four ingredients in large bowl.
2. Place 1 gallon bag in #10 can.
3. Pour curry mixture into bag, add remaining ingredients.
4. Seal bag, massage to combine; freeze.

To prepare: defrost completely. Place mixture in 8 x 8 oven proof pan. Cover with foil and bake 40 minutes. Remove foil, stir, bake 20 minutes more.

Serve with bread and salad

Serves: 6

Note: 1 boiled or pre-roasted chicken will give you 3 cups chopped chicken. This recipe can use up to 3 cups of chicken, if desired.

Grilled Seasoned Chicken

6 boneless skinless chicken breasts
½ cup prepared Italian salad dressing
¼ cup lemon juice
¼ cup balsamic vinegar
¼ cup olive oil
1 TSP garlic cloves, minced

1. Place bag in #10 can
2. Place chicken breasts in 1 gallon freezer bag.
3. Pour remaining ingredients over chicken.
4. Seal, shake to combine; freeze.

To prepare: Defrost mixture. Preheat grill or oven 350F.
Remove chicken from marinade and discard marinade. Cook on
grill 10 minutes, turn and cook additional 5 minutes or until
juices run clear.

Serve with spinach salad and cooked ziti tossed with butter and
garlic.

Serves: 6

Margarita Chicken

1 12 oz. can limeade, not reconstituted
$^2/_3$ cup tequila
1 bunch fresh cilantro
1 fresh jalapeno, seeded
6 boneless skinless chicken breasts

1. In blender container, add all ingredients except for chicken. Blend until well mixed.
2. Place 1 gallon freezer bag in #10 can
3. Add chicken and marinade.
4. Seal bag, shake to combine; freeze.

To prepare: Defrost mixture. Two cooking methods are available with this recipe. First – place chicken and marinade in large fry pan and cook all together. Alternately, remove chicken from marinade, reserve marinade – heat until boiling in small sauce pan. Cook chicken on barbecue until done, brushing with marinade, if already boiled.
If desired, cut chicken up. Place on salad greens, add additional toppings. Use cooked marinade for dressing.
Alternately, serve chicken and marinade over cooked quinoa.

Serves: 6

Mexican Chicken Lasagna

½ cup salsa
1 package taco seasoning
1 large egg
16 oz. ricotta cheese
2 garlic cloves, minced
10 uncooked lasagna
  noodles

3 cups cooked, cut up chicken
1 8 oz. can chopped green chilies
6 oz. grated Monterey Jack cheese
16 oz. can black beans, rinsed and
  drained
3 14 oz. cans stewed tomatoes with
  juice
¾ cup chopped onion, sautéed

1. Combine chopped onion with tomatoes, salsa and taco seasoning.
2. Whisk egg in small bowl with a fork, add ricotta cheese and garlic.
3. Spread 1 cup tomato sauce mixture over the bottom of greased 13 x 9 inch casserole. Top with 5 uncooked lasagna noodles.
4. Spread on one half of ricotta cheese mixture. Sprinkle with half the chicken and half the chilies.
5. Top with remaining tomato sauce, then ricotta cheese. Top with half of the cheese.
6. Top with remaining noodles, chicken, chilies, tomato sauce mixture and grated cheese. Cover and freeze.

To prepare: defrost completely. Heat oven to 350F. Remove lid, cover with foil Bake covered 60 minutes. Remove foil and bake an additional 20 minutes or until noodles are tender with pierced with sharp knife. Cool 10 minutes before serving.

Serve with salad.

Serves: 8

Note: 1 boiled or pre-roasted chicken will give you 3 cups chopped chicken. This recipe can use up to 3 cups of chicken, if desired.

Chicken Artichoke Casserole

½ cup butter
½ cup flour
1 ½ cups cream
1 ½ cups chicken broth (1 ½ TSP chicken bouillon and 1 ½ cups water)
½ TSP salt
1 TSP garlic
¼ TSP pepper
1 TSP rosemary
1 cup grated Parmesan cheese
1 cup mushrooms, canned
3 cups cooked, cut up chicken
2 cups artichoke hearts, drained

1. In large stock pot melt butter.
2. Stir in flour until well blended. Add cream and chicken broth.
3. Stir constantly over medium heat until thickened and flour taste is cooked out
4. Stir in garlic, salt, pepper, cheese and rosemary. Remove from heat and cool completely.
5. Place 1 gallon bag in #10 can.
6. Add mushroom, chicken and artichoke hearts.
7. When sauce is completely cooled, pour over chicken mixture.
8. Seal, shake to combine; freeze.

To prepare: Defrost mixture. Pour mixture into 8 x 8 oven proof dish. Bake at 325F for 30 minutes or until bubbly.
Serve over rice.

Serves: 6

Note: 1 boiled or pre-roasted chicken will give you 3 cups chopped chicken. This recipe can use up to 3 cups of chicken, if desired.

Port Marinated Top Sirloin

1 $1/_3$ cups port wine
2 carrots, sliced
2 shallots, sliced
3 garlic cloves, whole and peeled
1 TSP salt
1 TSP pepper
3 pounds top sirloin

1. Simmer all ingredients, except steak, in medium saucepan for 15 minutes. Removed from heat and cool completely.
2. Place 1 gallon freezer bag in #10 can.
3. Place meat in bag. Pour cooled marinade over steak.
4. Seal, shake to combine; freeze.

To prepare: Defrost mixture. Remove steak from marinade. Discard marinade. Barbecue meat until desired doneness is achieved. Alternately, broil steak in oven.

Serve with steamed green beans and baked potatoes.

Serves: 6

Brisket with Cranberry Gravy

3 pounds beef brisket
½ TSP salt
¼ TSP pepper
2 cups whole-berry cranberry sauce
1 cup tomato sauce
½ cup chopped onion, sautéed
1 TBSP chopped garlic.
1 TBSP Dijon mustard

1. Place 1 gallon bag in #10 can.
2. Place brisket in bag.
3. Add remaining ingredients.
4. Seal bag, massage to combine, freeze.

To prepare: Defrost mixture. Place entire mixture in crock pot.
Cover and cook on low for 8-10 hours or until meat is tender.
Remove brisket; thinly slice across the grain. Skim fat from
cooking juices; serve with brisket.
If desired – mix 1 TBSP flour with 2 TBSP water until well
blended, add to gravy and cook until thickened.
Serve with mashed potatoes and steamed peas.

Serves: 6

Five Bean Bake

½ cup onion, sautéed
1 pound ground beef, cooked (2 cups cooked)
2 15 oz. cans cut green beans
1 15 oz. can kidney beans
1 15 oz. can Great Northern Beans
1 15 oz. can black beans
1 15 oz. can pork and beans
2 cups honey Dijon barbecue sauce

Ingredients needed later
½ pound sliced bacon

If you followed the instructions at the beginning of the chapter, the onion and ground beef will be cooked, so start with step 2. If not, start at step 1.

1. Sauté onion and ground beef until done. Drain and cool.
2. Place 1 gallon freezer bag in #10 can.
3. Place onion, ground beef in bag. Open, drain and rinse all beans except pork and beans. Place all beans, including undrained pork and beans, in bag. Top with barbecue sauce.
4. Seal, shake to combine; freeze.

To prepare: Defrost mixture. Place in 9 x 13 baking dish. If desired, top with ½ pound sliced bacon. Bake at 350F for 45 minutes.

Serve with biscuits and salad.

Serves: 8

Stuffed Peppers

2 pounds ground beef, cooked and drained (4 cups cooked)
½ cup sautéed onion
2 cups uncooked rice – white or brown (yields 4 cups cooked)
2 15 oz. cans (4 cups) tomato sauce
½ TSP salt
½ TSP garlic powder
½ TSP pepper

Ingredients needed later
4 large green peppers
4 cups tomato sauce

If you followed the instructions at the beginning of the chapter, the onion, ground beef and rice will be cooked, so start with step 3. Otherwise, start at step 1.

1. Sauté ground beef and onion until done. Drain and cool completely.
2. Cook rice until done and cool completely.
3. Place all ingredients in large bowl and stir to combine.
4. Place 1 gallon freezer bag in #10 can.
5. Place all ingredients in bag. Seal, shake to combine; freeze.

To prepare: Defrost mixture. Cut tops off peppers and remove seeds. Place peppers in large saucepan, cover with water, bring to a boil; cook for 3 minutes. Drain and rinse in cold water; invert on paper towels.
Spoon beef mixture into peppers. Place in an ungreased shallow 2-qt. baking dish. Drizzle with remaining tomato sauce. Cover and bake at 350F for 25-30 minutes or until peppers are tender.
Alternately, use cabbage leaves – steam until soft – 3-4 minutes. Place meat mixture in cabbage leaves and roll up. Place seam side down in large baking dish, top with tomato sauce. Bake 25-30 minutes or until done.

Serve with salad and garlic bread.

Serves: 4

Montreal Flank Steak

2-3 pounds flank steak
½ cup water
½ cup soy sauce
2 TBSP brown sugar
2 TBSP lemon juice
2 TBSP red wine vinegar
2 TBSP vegetable oil
1 TBSP Montreal steak seasoning
½ TSP garlic powder
½ TSP hot pepper sauce
¼ TSP pepper

1. Place 1 gallon bags in #10 can.
2. Add flank steak.
3. Pour remaining ingredients over steak.
4. Seal, shake to combine; freeze.

To prepare: defrost completely. Remove steak from marinade and discard marinade. Heat barbecue to medium heat (350). Cook steak until desired doneness is achieved.

Serve with baked potatoes and salad.

Serves: 6

Sesame Beef Tenderloin

2-3 pounds beef tenderloin
¼ cup soy sauce
1 TSP ground ginger
1 TSP Dijon mustard
2 garlic cloves, minced

Ingredients needed later
¼ cup honey
2 TBSP sesame seeds

1. Place 1 gallon bag in #10 can.
2. Place tenderloin and remaining ingredients in bag.
3. Seal, shake to combine; freeze.

To prepare: Defrost completely. Drain and discard marinade. Brush beef with honey, sprinkle with sesame seeds. Place in shallow roasting pan. Bake at 400F for 25 minutes. Cover with foil. Bake 30 to 35 minutes longer or until meat reaches desired doneness. Let stand for 10 minutes before slicing.

Serve with stir fry vegetables and steamed rice that is tossed with sesame seeds.

Serves: 6

Easy Black Bean Chili

½ cup onion, sautéed
½ cup green bell pepper, sautéed
1 TBSP vegetable oil
2 garlic cloves, chopped
2 cans (15 oz. each) black beans, rinsed and drained
1 (28 oz.) can diced tomatoes, undrained
1 can (15 oz.) tomato sauce
1 TBSP chili powder
2 TSP cumin
2 TSP sugar

Optional ingredients
Sour cream
Fresh Cilantro

If you followed the instructions at the beginning of the chapter, the onion and green bell pepper will be cooked, start at step 2. If you did not follow the instructions, start at step 1.

1. Sauté onion and green bell pepper in vegetable oil.
2. Place 1 gallon bag in #10 can.
3. Pour all ingredients in to bag.
4. Seal, shake to combine; freeze.

To prepare: Defrost mixture. Place in large sauce pan, cover. Simmer over medium-low heat for 30 minutes. Top with sour cream and cilantro, if desired.

Serve with corn bread.

Serves: 6-8

Apricot-Glazed Pork Medallions

2 pounds pork tenderloin, cut crosswise into ½-inch thick rounds
2 ½ cups apricot preserves
½ cup tamari sauce (or soy sauce)
2 tablespoons chopped pickled ginger
  (fresh ginger will also work)

Ingredients Needed Later
4 teaspoons sesame oil

1. Place 1 gallon freezer bag in #10 can
2. Cut tenderloin, crosswise into ½ inch thick rounds
3. Place tenderloin in bag
4. In small bowl, blend remaining ingredients. Pour sauce over tenderloin.
5. Seal, shake to combine; freeze.

To prepare: Defrost mixture completely. Remove pork from marinade, reserve marinade. Heat oil in a large skillet over medium-high heat. Add pork and sear 2 minutes per side. Add marinade to pan, simmer 5 minutes, until pork is cooked through and sauce reduces.

Serve with steamed rice and stir fry vegetables

Serves: 6

Index

148

T

V

W

Z

www.ingramcontent.com/pod-product-compliance
Lightning Source LLC
LaVergne TN
LVHW021502080426
835509LV00018B/2377